THE WAY OF THE
WISEGUY

DONNIE BRASCO
(AKA JOSEPH D. PISTONE)

THE FBI'S MOST FAMOUS UNDERCOVER AGENT
CRACKS THE MOB MIND

RUNNING PRESS
PHILADELPHIA · LONDON

9   8   7
Digit on the right indicates the number of this printing

First paperback edition published in 2005

Library of Congress Control Number: 2003109166

ISBN-13 978-0-7624-2384-2
ISBN-10 0-7624-2384-6

Cover and interior design by Doogie Horner
Edited by Greg Jones
Audio CD produced by Sine Studios
Typography: Univers and Caslon

Front cover photos: AP/Wide World Photos. Vito Genovese (left), Al Capone (center top), Vincent Gigante (center middle), Joseph Bonanno (center bottom and right top), John Gotti (right bottom)

This book may be ordered by mail from the publisher.
Please include $2.50 for postage and handling.
But try your bookstore first!

Running Press Book Publishers
2300 Chestnut Street Suite 200
Philadelphia, PA 19103-4371

Visit us on the web!
www.runningpress.com

CONTENTS

ACKNOWLEDGMENTS

I just want to acknowledge all the fine agents of the FBI who put their lives on the line every day to keep the country safe.

FOREWORD

From Jesse James and Billy the Kid to Al Capone and John Gotti, Americans have always been fascinated with the outlaw. For decades, the larger than life bandit who flaunted his unconventional lifestyle has had a place in our pop culture. His fictionalized brother—Don Corleone or Tony Soprano for example—has added yet another layer of mystique. They've all become a part of Americana.

Hundreds of books and movies have capitalized on the desire of the average "citizen" to know more about what these guys are really like; why they do the things they do and what they think while they're doing them.

Presented in their most positive light, these wiseguys are either lovable rogues full of guile and panache or noble outcasts living by their own code of honor.

The reality, of course, is another story.

I've been writing about mobsters for more than twenty years. I've gotten to know more than a few. Many are now in jail. Others are dead. Some have stopped talking to me because of what I've had to say about them.

What I've picked up through all of that is one simple truth: there is no prototypical gangster. There are guys who are sharp and clever and fun to be around. Go out for dinner or drinks and you'll laugh all night. And there are guys who are somber and moody and full of themselves. Time spent with them can be excruciating . . . and also potentially dangerous.

There are wiseguys who are sophisticated and intelligent. There are others who are low-life thugs. Some are masters at making money. Others just know how to spend it. In other words, they're no different than any other group—doctors, lawyers, cops or reporters.

All of those guys are here, in Joe Pistone's fascinating new book, The Way of the Wiseguy. Pistone, the legendary FBI agent whose undercover life as "Donnie Brasco" has also become a part of Americana, knows the underworld as well as any made member of a crime family. He lived it for years. Ate, drank and slept it. Learned the language, and more important, the thought process behind it. Knew how to interpret a shrug, a nod or the fact that an associate was offering neither.

Pistone had to know all of this. His life depended on it.

To this day, because of the devastating effect his undercover work had on La Cosa Nostra, he has to live in an undisclosed location and under an assumed identity. The cases he made against the Colombo and Bonanno crime families were unprecedented and, twenty years later, are still having an impact.

This is the backstory to that undercover assignment and to years more of work in the underworld.

Whether it's a humorous anecdote about patriotism—a wiseguy once asked Pistone "When's the Fourth of July due" this year—or a realistic assessment of the underworld's definition of a "hostile takeover," Pistone delivers.

Clearly written, simply stated and full of unique insights, Pistone's take on La Cosa Nostra makes The Way of the Wiseguy a must-read for anyone interested in the American Mafia and how and why it has come apart at the seams. It is, among other things, the wiseguy's view of life, love, politics, government, relationships, food, respect and honor. And while Pistone understands it and can explain it better than anyone else in the business, it is important to remember that he never had any illusions about who these wiseguys were.

The product of the same kind of urban community that has

stocked the mob for three generations, Joe Pistone always knew whom he was dealing with. They were the dark-side of the Italian-American experience. They took the positive values of that community—honor, family and loyalty—and bastardized them to their criminal ends.

"There is no honor among these thieves," Pistone told a U.S. Senate Subcommittee back in 1988, while recounting his undercover exploits as Donnie Brasco. "They deal in drugs, death and deception."

—GEORGE ANASTASIA
October 2004

INTRODUCTION

It is me and Lefty Guns in a hotel bar in Miami Beach. Tourists, tacky decor, and women with scary tans. Lefty is my Mafia mentor, the Bonanno family soldier who is educating me in the conduct expected of a mobster. Me, I'm a good listener. So we're sitting there having a few drinks and talking about this and that, when it occurs to me to ask Lefty what I think is a pretty good question.

"Hey, Lefty? What's the advantage for me in being a wiseguy?"

Lefty looks at me like I'm the world's biggest moron. He gets excited and jumps out of his chair and starts yelling and waving his arms. "What are you, fucking crazy?" he says. "Are you fucking nuts? When you're a wiseguy, you can steal, you can cheat, you can lie, you can kill people—and it's all legitimate."

That, in a nutshell, is the way of the wiseguy: Whatever crazy stuff you do, whatever racket you are into, it is all legitimate. The wiseguy does not see himself as a criminal or even a bad person; he sees himself as a businessman, a shrewd hustler, one step ahead of ordinary suckers. The wiseguy lives by a vastly different set of rules than those observed by regular people, rules that were fashioned by their criminal forefathers and proven to work by generations of mobsters before them. Wiseguys exist in a bizarre parallel universe, a world where avarice and violence and corruption are the norm, and where the routines that most ordinary people hold dear—working good jobs, being with family, living an honest life—are seen as the curse of the weak and the stupid. Wiseguys resemble us in many ways, but make no mistake: they might as well be from another planet, so alien and abnormal are their thoughts and habits.

I know something about the way of the wiseguy. I know more than most people about what makes wiseguys tick. The reason I do is because I was once a wiseguy myself.

The truth is I was only pretending to be a wiseguy. In reality, I was a Special Agent of the Federal Bureau of Investigation. As such I infiltrated numerous groups of wiseguys all over the world, and came to know their ways and means. I've worked with Scotland Yard, penetrated the Chinese Triads, ran undercover operations in a bunch of third world countries, and busted bad guys all over America. My most memorable assignment, however, was to go deep undercover into a New York Mafia family. And so I became Donnie Brasco, jewel thief. The operation was one of the most successful undercover stings in the history of the FBI, and you could say that I "wrote the book" on how to infiltrate the mob. In fact, my account of that operation, *Donnie Brasco*, became a *New York Times* bestseller as well as a feature film starring Johnny Depp and Al Pacino. Johnny Depp, of course, played me, Donnie Brasco.

As Donnie, I lived the life of a wiseguy, becoming an associate of the Bonanno crime family, one of the five major families in New York. I was part of a well-respected crew, and I partook in nearly every facet of wiseguy life. I spent twenty-four hours a day, seven days a week being Donnie Brasco. Most undercover assignments last six months. I was able to convince hard-core gangsters for six years that I was one of them.

I am still the only undercover FBI agent to ever be proposed for membership in a Mafia family. I came within four months of becoming a made man.

Once my cover was purposefully blown, I testified at dozens of trials, including the infamous "Pizza Connection" heroin-smuggling case and the "Mafia Commission" trial of the mob's entire ruling body. My testimony helped secure more than one hundred federal convictions against wiseguys. And combined with the aggressive tactics of other law enforcement agencies, the impact of my exposure of the mob's rules and customs forever changed the way wiseguys do business. It is safe to say that Donnie Brasco dealt a serious and damaging blow to the American Mafia.

And yet I was not naïve enough then, nor am I now, to believe that we came anywhere near to destroying the mob and ending organized crime. It is true that the Mafia today is not nearly as strong or far-reaching as it was only two or three decades ago, that its top bosses are all dead or in jail, that more turncoats are breaking their vows of *omerta* than ever before, that "disorganized crime" is more like it, given the sorry state of mob leadership.

But that doesn't mean that the Mafia is dead and buried. Far from it.

The mob and mobsters have been around for centuries, and they will almost certainly be around for many generations to come. As long as there is money to be made illicitly and with minimal investment, there will be wiseguys ready and willing to make the score. The fact is that the Mafia in particular is one of the most enduring and successful organizations in the history of the world. There has never been a corporation that lasted as long or changed as little as the Mafia, which dates back to the 1800s. What's more, the Mafia has never had a single year out of decades when it ran in the red. The Mafia always makes a profit. There is a strong incentive for wiseguys to keep things running in the black: deficits mean death.

Yes, wiseguys are a fascinating breed, and the rules and codes they live by, while easily defined, are perhaps difficult to imagine following yourself. Me, I got to see how they live up close, and, as both an FBI agent and a mob soldier, I have a pretty unique perspective on wiseguys. Working undercover as a mobster—in effect, acting like a wiseguy—required me to pay extra attention to what they did and how they did it, to study them and soak up their ways and then spit them back out. If you are intrigued by the mob way of life, if you find the conduct and charisma of these guys darkly fascinating, then the stories I have to tell will be of interest to you. I penetrated into the very heart of the Mafia and lived to tell about it.

Chances are that in your lifetime you will have at least one brush with the Mafia or some other wiseguy. Maybe you'll unknow-ingly eat in a mob-connected restaurant. Maybe prices in your local store will go up because of the mob stealing merchandise. Maybe you'll buy scalped tickets from some half-ass wiseguy. Maybe you'll make a bet with some guy named Knuckles. Unless you spend your whole life holed up somewhere in Iowa, chances are you will at least rub up against one of the Mafia's many expansive tentacles. Wiseguys are everywhere, walking among us; a little more inclined to brazenly double-park, perhaps, but part of the fabric of society, nonetheless.

You can either look away and pretend they don't exist, or you can take a good, hard look and understand what's what. I had no choice but to immerse myself in the wiseguy culture—it was my job to infiltrate their society and get as many of them off the streets as I could. And, anyway, I'm not the type to bury my head in the sand about anything. You want to know about wiseguys—about real wiseguys and not those cuddly wiseguys you see on TV and in movies? Fine. I can tell you a thing or two about them. You have come to the right place, my friends.

• • • • •

I have been around wiseguys all my life. I grew up around them on the streets of the Sandy Hill section of Paterson, New Jersey. As I got older, I worked all kinds of blue-collar jobs: in con-struction, in bars, driving tractor trailers. For some reason, though, I had this idea that I could be an FBI agent. There were no cops or feds in my family, no role models who pushed me into law enforcement. It was just this thing I had. My first government job was with the Office of Naval Intelligence, investigating drug, theft, and espionage cases. But after that, I passed the FBI's entrance exams and became a Special Agent in 1969. Very quickly, my specialty became clear: I was very proficient in street work.

Maybe it was my appearance, maybe my accent, maybe it was the way I handled myself. Whatever it was, I just had a knack for making reliable street contacts. Certainly I respected street guys, because I was one myself. In my early years in the Bureau, working out of Jacksonville, Florida, I ran up against petty crooks, prostitutes, pimps, hijackers, drug addicts, and flat-out killers. My dealings with these denizens of a dark and dirty underworld prepared me well for what lay ahead—for when I became Donnie Brasco and signed up with the mob.

In fact, I first assumed the identity of Donald Brasco, a name I remembered from an old book or movie, to work with the Truck and Hijack Squad and go undercover in an operation to bust a truck-hijacking ring. My success at infiltrating and bringing down the ring—we arrested something like thirty hard-core truck boosters—caught the eye of my superiors at the Bureau, who called on me again when they needed someone to go undercover as a fence for goods stolen by wiseguys. Little did I know that when I accepted that assignment, my life would never be the same—not even close.

And so I erased my real identity, as Joseph Pistone, Special Agent for the FBI, and became one Donnie Brasco, small-time jewel thief from the West Coast. When I say I erased my identity, I mean I obliterated it. I plunged so deeply undercover that I did not set foot in an FBI office for the entire six years of the operation. The people I worked with, the friends I had made over the years, had no clue what happened to me. Not even my wife knew the full story of what I was doing. Essentially, I was an army of one taking on the dreaded Mafia, without so much as a guy backing me in the street should things go wrong. Had I been arrested, the FBI would have denied any knowledge of me or the operation. I was, for all practical purposes, a wiseguy.

Fortunately, I was good at it. I started by hanging out at Carmello's, a wiseguy hangout in the Yorkville section of Manhattan. Not doing anything, just hanging out, becoming a familiar face. I played backgammon with a few regulars, got introduced around as "Don," finally got around to trying to sell some "hot" rings and wristwatches to the bartender. Eventually I met some connected guys, some half-ass wiseguys, and then some real mafioso. I got in good with some wiseguys from the Colombo crime family, and worked it so that I always did things like unload stolen merchandise, but never went out on jobs myself. I became this quiet, useful guy to have around. Through my Colombo contacts I met Tony Mirra, a member of the Bonanno family. And through Mirra I met Benjamin "Lefty Guns" Ruggiero, another Bonanno soldier. Lefty would be the wiseguy who would vouch for me and bring me fully into the Bonanno family. He was also my professor at Wiseguy University: from him, I learned the ins and outs of being a true wiseguy.

For the next several years, I did not exist except as a close associate of several members of the Bonanno crime family. There was no facet of the wiseguy life that I was not exposed to. I became a trusted friend of capo Dominick "Sonny Black" Napolitano and got to meet big-time Florida mobster Santo Trafficante. I will not deny that I became pretty close to a lot of these wiseguys, and that I felt a pang of remorse about doing things that I knew would get them killed. But it was only a pang. The truth is that I did not feel sorry for the wiseguys I helped put away. Had they discovered that I was an undercover FBI agent, they would have put two in my head and chopped me into ground beef. Instead, I made it through undetected and did what I had to do as a law enforcement officer. In the end, some wiseguys went so far as to say I had been a stand-up guy, that they did not hold what I had done against me. Of course, at the same time, the Mafia Commission put a $500,000 contract on my head. Like Michael Corleone said, "It's not personal; it's just business."

Much later, after breaking my Donnie Brasco cover, I would testify before a Senate subcommittee as something of an expert on the Mafia. Certainly, I learned everything I needed to make a convincing wiseguy, and that information about the subculture of mobsters has helped the FBI in its continuing war against the Mafia. My book, *Donnie Brasco*, is still used by the FBI as a sort of handbook on undercover operations and the mob.

What, then, came of all that, of the risks to my safety and family that I repeatedly took? What was accomplished by my unprecedented infiltration of a crime family? Did I really change anything by becoming a wiseguy for six years? Hey, let's leave it to the historians to figure that out. I got some wiseguys off the street, built up the FBI's store of information about mob culture, laid the groundwork for future undercover operations and, at least in a small way, convinced the government that the war against the Mafia is, indeed, winnable. Tough and resilient and indestructible as wiseguys may seem, they can be brought down. It takes time, guts, and street smarts, but it can be done.

● ● ● ● ●

Not that I expect that to happen in our lifetime. As I said, wiseguys have incredible instincts for survival, and their way of life perpetuates itself with every crooked deal. Quite frankly, their way works, and so they stick with it. This book, in the end, is an inside look at this unique subculture, stories of how wiseguys live and work and waste time and reach for power and kill each other like they're scratching an itch. It's a descent into a strange and dangerous world, one best observed from a safe distance. The things I saw were disturbing, funny, eye-opening, sad, a little bit of everything. In other words, life, wiseguy-style.

So take it for what you will. It is what it is. Me, I make no claims. All I can tell you is that I was once a wiseguy. And that it was a hell of a time.

1

WISEGUYS ARE NOT NICE GUYS

This one poor bastard, he did something to make wiseguys think he was a rat. So they stuck a meat hook up his ass and hung him from a warehouse wall.

While he was alive.

I tell you this to drive home the most important observation I ever made while working undercover: Wiseguys are not nice guys. Wiseguys aren't even close to being nice guys. In fact, wiseguys are the meanest, cruelest, least caring people you'll ever meet. They have zero regard for other people's feelings, rights, and safety. They will end your life with all the forethought required to flick off a light switch.

Wiseguys are barbaric. They may seem funny, endearing, and even admirable on TV, but that is fiction. In real life, wiseguys are capable of unbelievable atrocities. This other guy, a connected guy, he made the mistake of running his mouth and disrespecting certain wiseguys. They cut off his dick and stuffed it in his mouth and left him to die in the street.

The history of the Mafia is a history of bloodshed and murder. Consider the poor bastard who ran afoul of some members of the Gambino crime family. They cut some holes in him, hung him over a bathtub, and drained all the blood out of his body. These are not rare occurrences or unusual crimes. Wiseguys routinely commit acts of nauseating grisliness. Forget about when someone is already dead and they cut up his body with chain saws and butcher knives like they were carving a side of beef. We're talking about what they do to people when they are still alive. All sorts of body parts are cut off— ears, tongues, hands, feet, and, of course, dicks. Eyes have been gouged out, heads caved in, bones sledge-hammered, and bodies crushed. Weapons include golf clubs, steel bars, brass knuckles, baseball bats. Blood literally runs in little rivers when wiseguys decide to use knives and even swords. Guns, of course, are the most common weapon, and the most humane. A couple of quick ones to the back of the head makes you one of the lucky ones. It means you didn't live long enough to experience having your genitals served to you for lunch.

Wiseguys have cast-iron stomachs when it comes to the grisly work of murder. I remember when Caesar Bonventre got whacked. He was one of the guys who set up Carmine Galante, one of the most famous mob rubouts ever. But Bonventre was a Sicilian, a zip, and as such, he was not as highly regarded as wiseguys from the U.S. After Galante, Bonventre got a little too cocky, tried to exert his authority a little too much, stepped out of line a bit. The order came down to whack him, and he got shot and killed. Then some wiseguys tried to dispose of his body by running it through a meat grinder. They fed the body into the grinder and listened to the saws tear through flesh and bone. Blood and bits of brain flying everywhere. But then the body got struck. It was simply too big to get all the way through. The wiseguys pushed and pushed, but the saws locked up and Bonventre's body was sticking halfway out of the grinder, the legs dangling in the air. The wiseguys had to pull out this chewed-up body, which was now in bloody pieces. They wound up sticking the body into three different oil drums filled with glue. That's the stuff of nightmares for most people, but wiseguys do it routinely without batting an eye. Wiseguys don't throw up or even gag when they butcher people. They have had any decency and sense of revulsion bred right out of them.

Of course, wiseguys are in the business of killing people who cross them, so it's hardly surprising that they would come up with some pretty imaginative ways to do it. But murdering people is not the only way wiseguys reveal their evil character. Wiseguys beat up a lot more people than they kill. I accompanied Tony Mirra, a particularly surly wiseguy, to collect from some guy who had borrowed money. I knew the guy was having trouble paying, and I knew that Tony had the heart to really put this guy through hell. We approach him, and he's maybe three seconds away from multiple concussions when I step in and tell Tony that I'm going to take the guy for a walk. Tony lets me do it, so I walk the guy a few hundred yards away and give him a minor beating. I didn't feel good about beating him up at all, considering that I was a federal law enforcement officer, but I also knew that if I hadn't stepped in, he would have received a beating that was ten times worse. That's the thing with wiseguys: they have absolutely no problem at all working somebody over if that somebody owes them money or otherwise fucked up on a deal. They do not hesitate to break somebody's arms and legs, because doing so, in the world of wiseguys, is good business. Wiseguys take care of their own problems—they do not go to police to settle disputes or complain about being mistreated. They go out and handle things themselves. Say what you will about wiseguys, they take care of business. They will inflict whatever harm is necessary to achieve their bottom line, which is get the money they came to get.

Wiseguys are not mean and violent just during work hours. Wiseguys are pretty much pricks all day long. At any point on any given day, they can turn from being mellow to menacing in the blink of an eye. I remember riding in a car with a bunch of wiseguys when this unlucky bastard pulled up behind us at a stoplight and inadvertently bumped into our car. I mean, the guy tapped us with his bumper. Anyone else, you shrug it off and go on your way. At worst, you turn around and give the guy a nasty look. But not wiseguys. A couple of seconds after the guy bumped us, all of us got out of the car like he had slapped our mothers on the mouth. I stood there watching as the wiseguys ripped open the guy's front door, pulled him out of the car, and beat the living shit out of him. They punched him repeatedly in the face, breaking his nose and splitting his lips. They kicked him in the stomach and head when he fell to the ground. Me, I couldn't just stand there and let them kill this fellow for bumping into our car, so I reached down and tried to break it up. That's when one of the wiseguys started punching me in the face for taking sides against other mobsters. I couldn't lay a finger on the guy, because I knew he was made. So I took my beating along with the guy on the ground.

Wiseguys, you see, are not nice guys.

This sort of thing went on all the time. This other instance, me and Lefty were driving up Third Avenue when a taxi cut us off, not once but twice. After the second time, when we stopped at a light, Lefty got out, popped the trunk, retrieved a tire iron and smashed the guy's front window. Then he got back in the car and we drove off. The guy cut us off, Lefty smashed his window. Makes perfect sense in the world of the wiseguy.

Beyond this propensity for violence and mayhem, I saw plenty of evidence that wiseguys are seriously lacking in humanity. There was this black guy who ran numbers for us up in Harlem, and he would come down to Little Italy once a week to settle up. But the wiseguys would never let the guy inside their social club, because they had a strict rule barring blacks from the club. So they would make the guy stand outside until they were ready to do business with him and collect his tally sheets. That was bad enough in itself, but it got worse. No matter what the weather, they made this guy wait outside. Some days it rained sheets; some days it snowed; some days it was absolutely freezing; and still, they made him wait outside. When the weather was really bad, they made him wait even longer—an hour or more. And they got a good laugh out of making him wait.

I could go on about wiseguys not being nice guys, but I think I've made my point. I don't want anybody getting the wrong idea. I spent a lot of years around wiseguys and I know them pretty good.

There is nothing romantic about them or what they do. Understand what we're talking about here—bad, bad men. Are they funny? Sure. Kind to their mothers and children? You bet. Generous to the help? You bet. But the same day they tip the valet $100 they might stick a meat hook up a guy's ass.

2

WISEGUYS MEAN BUSINESS

Know this about wiseguys: they play for keeps. No second chances, no reprieves, no trial runs. You fuck up, you pay the price, and the price is very steep. Wiseguys live lives that resemble yours and mine in many ways except for this: they live under the constant threat of being clipped. Their decisions, concerns, actions are all magnified one hundred times by the reality that mistakes mean death. The Mafia could not exist without its rules and codes of conduct, which are rigidly enforced and never open to question. In life, you break the social contract—such as speeding in your car—and you get a fine. In business, you make a mistake, maybe you get demoted or fired. Even in the army, you have military tribunals through which you can maybe beat the rap. But when you're a wiseguy facing wiseguy justice, there is no lawyer to defend you, no procedure in place to protect your rights. Your life is now in someone else's hands, and you know it. Wiseguys wake up every day, aware that this may be the day that they get killed, at any moment, for lots of different reasons. It is a simple fact of life in the wiseguy world. It comes with the territory.

Take the case of the wiseguys I worked with while I was undercover as Donnie Brasco. They were guilty of one of the worst transgressions imaginable in the Mafia: they allowed an undercover federal agent to infiltrate the family. Sonny Black took me around to other bosses and introduced me as "a friend of ours." He took me to no less a boss than Santo Trafficante down in Tampa and completely vouched for me. Tony Mirra did the same thing, introducing me to Junior Persico. Lefty Ruggiero took me to meet Milwaukee boss, Frank Balistrieri. These were bosses from other families who had no way of knowing if I was a made guy; they had to depend entirely on the word and judgment of the wiseguys who vouched for me.

Then it came out that I was undercover, and, as wiseguys like to say, "the fan hit the shit." Seventeen days after Donnie Brasco was exposed as an FBI agent, Sonny Black was called to a sit-down. He went into the Motion Lounge in Brooklyn and had a drink with the bartender, Charlie. Then he calmly took off his rings, his watch, his crucifix, and handed them to Charlie, along with his apartment keys. He got up to leave with only some money in his pocket and his car keys. "I gotta go," he told Charlie, "and I'm probably not coming back."

Sonny disappeared after that. Months later, they found his body in a body bag underneath the Verrazano Bridge, on the Staten Island side. Both of his hands had been cut off. The message was clear. Sonny had introduced me to bosses, had me shake their hands. So he lost his, plain and simple.

A few months after that, it was Tony Mirra's turn. Mirra was in his car in the parking garage of a high-rise apartment down by the river in Manhattan when he got shot. He was left in the car, slumped and bleeding. He had thousands of dollars still in his pockets, so cops knew it wasn't a robbery. Leaving his body to be found was a message to other wiseguys to be more careful.

Lefty Ruggiero, the wiseguy I was closest to, was set to be clipped, too. But we picked up the hit on a wiretap, and we managed to arrest Lefty as he was on his way to get whacked. Otherwise, it would have been a clean sweep, a total bloodbath, all caused by Donnie Brasco. As it was, this was the first time two such big mobsters—Sonny was a capo, and Mirra was a highly respected wiseguy—got killed over an undercover FBI agent. After that, the Mafia changed its rule about vouching for new members. After Donnie Brasco, a newcomer had to be vouched for by two wiseguys, not just one.

Me, I knew these guys would get killed when I came out. Like I said, I felt maybe a pang of regret that what I had done led people to lose their lives, but it was only a tiny fucking pang. These guys knew as well as anybody that what happened meant they would be killed. It may have taken a day or two to dawn on them, to realize they had fucked up in the worst possible way. But they knew deep down that allowing me to infiltrate the family was a sin they would pay for with their lives. That was just the reality of the situation. They knew this, and yet they did nothing to prevent it. They could have disappeared, moved to Russia or something. They certainly could have flipped and gone into a program. Yet they stuck around, didn't try to hide. This, they knew, was the way of the wiseguy. You cannot change it, you cannot fight it. You just deal with it. When you are in the life, you accept death. That's just the way it is.

3

WHY WISEGUYS WILL KILL YOU

This wiseguy I knew, his captain called him and gave him the contract to kill a man. The captain explained that the man had raped another man's daughter. All the wiseguy knows of his target is that he is a chef at a fancy restaurant. So the wiseguy goes into the place, asks where the chef is, goes back into the kitchen and approaches a guy in a big chef's hat. "Are you so and so?" he asks the chef. The chef says, "Yes, I am." The wiseguy puts two bullets in his head, right in front of the entire kitchen staff. Chef goes down; wiseguy walks out. End of story.

Wiseguys do not like rape. If you rape someone who is a relative of a made guy or someone with some ties to the mob, you are in big trouble, and I'm not talking about the cops or courts. Wiseguys have a pretty low threshold for what is and isn't decent, but the crime of rape is one of the few transgressions that does not meet that threshold. This chef, he happened to rape someone who knew someone in the mob, and it got him killed.

The thing is, wiseguys do not go around killing people for no good reason. Like I said, if you read in the paper about some guy getting whacked, it's a really good bet he was either a made guy who somehow fucked up, or some poor guy who got in over his head with wiseguys and paid the ultimate price, or, in the case of the chef, a guy who did something that is not tolerated in the orbit of wiseguys. It is very unusual for people with no mob dealings or no connection to the mob to wind up dead at the hands of a mobster.

If, however, you are a wiseguy or a guy with some association to the mob, and you do certain things, you will get whacked. There are certain mob rules that must never, ever be broken. They are not hard to understand, and there is no mystery to them at all—they are laid out for you going in so that you will not break them by accident. These are the things that will get you whacked by a wiseguy:

Not sharing money from illegal activities will get you killed. If you are a guy whose business is being protected by the mob, to hold out on them or to try to hide some cash is a capital offense. If you are a wiseguy, everything you gain illegally, all your extorted monies, must be shared with your captain and your partners in your crew. To pocket money on the side or not declare everything you make is to flirt with the most gruesome death imaginable.

Testifying before a grand jury will get you killed. If summoned, you got to go, but once you're there, do not testify. The last thing in the world you want to do is testify against mobsters, unless you are ready to enter witness protection and never speak to any of your loved ones again.

Talking to cops will get you killed. Anything more than, "Nice day, officer," is grounds for execution.

Laying your hands on another wiseguy will get you killed. It's a pretty simple rule—you never go after another wiseguy without the full and clear blessing of the bosses. Stay away from any physical confrontations with other wiseguys, and always stick up for wiseguys in any beef against a normal citizen. Punching out a wiseguy because he pissed you off or called your girlfriend a name could very well get you killed.

Speaking of girlfriends, the quickest way to catch two in the head is to mess around with a wiseguy's girlfriend, wife, or daughter. That is maybe the dumbest thing you could ever do. Fucking a wiseguy's woman is a huge transgression and one from which it is almost impossible to recover. Even if a wiseguy has broken up with a girlfriend and hasn't seen her for several months, do not try to fuck her. Run from her like she's got the plague. Find another broad. Messing around with a wiseguy's girl will get you killed.

Apparently, being gay will get you killed, too. Johnny Boy D'Amato, acting consigliere of New Jersey's DeCavalcante crime family, was shot to death because his girlfriend passed it around that she thought he was gay. The family, fearing it would become a laugh-ingstock if word got out that its consigliere was gay, gave the contract to DeCavalcante soldier Anthony Capo, who dutifully shot Johnny Boy. So, being gay is not necessarily good for your health in the wiseguy world.

Breaking any of these rules does not automatically mean that you will be whacked. It will simply subject you to possibly getting killed. And the jury that will consider your case is a bunch of wiseguys sitting around a table who care more about what's for din-ner that night than they do about your life. So be a smart wiseguy, and never, ever break these golden rules.

Then again, you might wind up breaking one without even knowing you are doing it. This one wiseguy's captain called him one time to give him the contract to kill this other man—an unconnected guy. Seems the man was in a poker game and lost all his money, but, being the lousy and degenerate gambler he was, could not pull him-self away from the table. Instead, he decided to gamble his wife. Told the guys, "If I lose, you can fuck my wife." Sure enough, the guy lost, and then showed up at his home with the winner by his side. Tells his wife, "Honey, I lost at cards, so now you have to fuck this guy." His dutiful wife did as she was asked—or ordered. But the next day, she told her brother, who was friends with a wiseguy. The wiseguy told his captain, and the hit was ordered. The degenerate gambler answered the doorbell one day and got two to the head.

There is no specific wiseguy rule against gambling your wife in a poker game. But you should know that ordering your wife to fuck a guy to whom you owe money is the sort of thing that wiseguys do not like. Unless you are absolutely positive that your wife has no con-nection to the Mafia, even three or four times removed, do yourself a favor and do not bet her in a poker hand. The stakes, my friend, are higher than you can imagine.

4

WISEGUYS
AND MONEY

One time, I needed to collect a debt from a wiseguy who owned a car wash. I go over to this guy's establishment and he ushers me into a back room, where there is a row of lockers, maybe six-feet-high by six-feet-wide. The guy goes over to one of the lockers and opens it up. The thing is fucking stuffed with cash. I mean, it is packed to the top with stacks of tens and twenties and hundreds. Turns out every single locker is similarly jammed with dough. The guy reaches in, pulls out a bundle, counts out ten grand, and hands it over to me.

He has just made a withdrawal from a wiseguy bank.

Money is absolutely everything to wiseguys, the very reason for their existence, and it is not surprising that the way they think about and handle money is different from what most people are used to. When you're a criminal involved in criminal enterprises every single day of your life, you have to be extremely smart and crafty when it comes to keeping, accounting for, investing, and spending your money. The alternative to shrewd management of your finances is jail or death.

The golden rule of wiseguy finance is this—it's all cash. Wiseguys do not have bank accounts or checkbooks or IRAs or ATM cards. They have big fucking stacks of cold hard cash. They keep their cash in all sorts of places—in a safe in their home or office, in a shoebox hidden in the ceiling, deep inside an underwear drawer. One place they don't keep their money is a bank. Why the fuck would a wiseguy want to have thousands of dollars in some fucking bank? So the feds can take it when they pinch you for extortion? The most important thing a wiseguy must do with his money is hide it.

Of course, some wiseguys have to have bank accounts. Maybe they run a legitimate business that requires a bank account and checks; maybe they run a sham business that also requires access to a bank. If a wiseguy absolutely needs to have a bank account, you can be damned sure that the account will not be in the wiseguy's name. It will be in his mother's name or his father's name or in the name of a brother or a cousin. Maybe a wiseguy's wife will the official bearer of the funds. Anybody is fine, as long as it's not the wiseguy himself. Wiseguys cannot, under any circumstances, allow any connection to be drawn between themselves and their money. If the shit comes down and the feds move in, the first thing they will take is your money—if they can link it to you. Wiseguys never need their cash more than when they are hauled off to jail, to pay for lawyers and send to their wives and all that. So it is vital that the money be untouchable—and in somebody else's name.

Cash is hardly the only asset that mobsters carefully conceal. A clever wiseguy can be very wealthy *and* own nothing. A car? Wiseguys will make sure their cars are purchased by someone else and registered in someone else's name. Again, your mother or wife or cousin is ideal. A house? Wiseguys never buy houses outright. The mortgage is taken out by a relative, so that the true ownership of the house is not a matter of public record. Most people spend their lives accumulating assets and getting their names listed on more and more public documents—mortgages, automobile titles, long-term CDs, on and on. Wiseguys spend their lives divesting themselves of as many assets as they can. The older a wiseguy gets, the less stuff he is likely to have his name on. Some wiseguys are so stealthy when it comes to hiding assets, you would be hard-pressed to find a single mention of them in any public record. They are absolute ghosts, phantoms. The richest fucking wiseguy in the world may not have put his name on a check in decades.

There are many advantages to running a business this way. For instance, owning an enterprise that is entirely cash-driven means you don't have to pay a fucking dime in taxes. After all, you have to cut your bosses in for as much as eighty percent of what you make, and that means there is very little left over for Uncle Sam. Even so, wiseguys are not too worried about the IRS. Again, most people live in fear of the IRS, absolutely tremble at the thought of an audit. Wiseguys could care less if the IRS is up their ass. I have seen wiseguys get IRS notices in the mail and just crumple them up and throw them in the trash. What do they care if they get audited? Wiseguys live with the chance that they might get whacked any fucking minute—you think they're going to be intimidated when some IRS agent shows up? The guy could be the best agent in the history of the IRS, and he still won't be able to make any sense of a wiseguy's finances. His head will fucking explode if he tries to establish a money trail. Yes, it's true that Al Capone was finally brought down by an IRS agent. But, believe me, wiseguys will take their chances with the IRS any day of the week. They will likely be dead or in jail on another offense long before the IRS figures out what to charge them with.

The truth is, the IRS doesn't have a chance against wiseguys, because it is next to impossible to keep track of the cash that keeps the Mafia running. Money comes, money goes, and nobody keeps receipts. Some wiseguys, in rare circumstances, might use credit cards. Maybe they pay for this and that with the credit card registered to their sham business. Also, some wiseguys use credit cards that are fraudulently manufactured or stolen. But, for the most part, all bills will be paid for with bills. You go to a restaurant with eight or ten other wiseguys, you run up a huge tab, you get the check, and you pull out a three-inch-thick roll of Lincolns and Hamiltons. No muss, no fuss. Nothing is cleaner to use than dirty money.

The almost exclusive use of cash by wiseguys puts them at odds with the average citizen who on any given day might not even touch a dollar bill, relying on ATM and credit cards for every purchase. But that is only one way that the mob economy differs from that of the general public. In most business, revenues are gathered by the corporate brass, who then distributes it to payroll, who then passes it along to the workers. The money flows down. But in the mob, the exact opposite is true.

In the world of the wiseguy, all the money flows up. Revenue comes in through the very bottom tier. A variety of scams are run by associates and soldiers, producing a consistent stream of income. That income is then funneled upstairs to the higher-ups. Specifically, an associate has to kick a healthy share of his loot to a soldier, and the soldier has to kick some of his take to the captain. In turn, the captain has to make a weekly payment into the boss's kitty. The flow of money rarely deviates from this upward trajectory. What varies is the percentage of your bounty you get to keep. That depends on how greedy the guy is above you.

Say an associate gets his hands on some hot merchandise and fences it for a nice little score of a few thousand bucks. He is going to kick a big chunk of that to the soldier who is above him in the crew. An associate can show some initiative and come up with his own scams and make money on his own. But under no circumstances can he then keep all that money for himself. Holding out on any earnings from any job is an offense that may very well get you killed. All money earned by a wiseguy is subject to being divided among the wiseguys above you.

So the associate hands over, say fifty percent of his haul. Some soldiers will ask for less, some for more. Then the soldier scoops up the few hundred he made from that soldier, adds it up with the money he made from other associates and from his own scams, and hands over a percentage of that sum to his captain. Again, some captains will ask for fifty percent, others will let you keep a little more. Generally, it is on a score-by-score basis. Even if you make a hundred dollars on some scam, you go to your captain and you allow him to take what he wants. If he's a decent guy, he'll take ten bucks and let you keep the rest. Greedy bastards will take fifty percent of whatever is waved under their noses. But, as a wiseguy, you know that going in—the money always flows up.

So, now the captain has taken his cut of the earnings of all the soldiers and associates in his crew. Out of that figure, he must produce the amount that is requested of him by the boss of the family every week. All the captains of the family must make weekly payments to the boss, and the amount of those payments is completely at the whim and discretion of the boss. Maybe he tells his captain he needs to have twenty thousand dollars in an envelope every Friday. Maybe he then surprises a captain by upping that amount to twenty-five thousand dollars without warning. The captain has to produce that envelope every single week, without fail. When he falls short, the captain usually goes nuts and terrorizes his soldiers and demands they increase their payments to him. I remember Sonny Black going ballistic on a number of occasions, all because the boss kept putting pressure on him to keep the money coming. He, in turn, would chew out his guys and scare them into bringing in more dough. There is no such thing in the Mafia world as a sluggish economy. You will never hear mobsters say they had a weak fiscal quarter. This series of payments that mobsters make to their superiors is absolutely relentless and irrespective of the state of the legitimate economy. If you're a captain, you better find some way to make your weekly payment—if you don't, you're not going to be a captain for too long.

And so it goes—the money comes in, the money flows up. No Mafia boss is out there earning money and distributing it downward to his loyal subordinates. The grunts are the ones who have to sweat it out and send it up. Again, this system keeps the hands of the higher-ups as clean as possible. There is no questioning it, no challenging it, no suggesting alternative methods. There is only blind and slavish allegiance to the wiseguy way.

So what is it that wiseguys do with all that cash they get to keep? Depends on the wiseguy. Some become degenerate gamblers and waste every dime betting on horses. Some are cheap bastards and save as much as they can. Some like to lavish money on their women. Some of the younger wiseguys are drug addicts who spend a bundle getting high. Some are family men who take their kids to Disney World. I guess, in that way, wiseguys are no different from anyone else. That is, if you call pulling wads of money out of shoeboxes normal.

5

GAMBLING AND LOAN-SHARKING

Of all the various scams and operations orchestrated by wiseguys, none is as profitable and as dependable as illegal gambling. There are a couple of reasons for this. The first and foremost is that the world is full of lousy, degenerate gamblers. Absolutely crawling with guys who would bet their grandmother's last set of dentures on the outcome of the Florida–Florida State game. Another reason why gambling is such a successful enterprise for wiseguys is that it is a 365-day-a-year proposition. Again, this is because people who are addicted to gambling do it every single fucking day they can. Stocks schemes, chop shops, construction sites— they all shut down eventually, for a day or a week or a month, whatever. But the gambling never, ever stops. There is always—always— something for a degenerate gambler to bet on. Baseball, basketball, hockey, the horses—it's the wide fucking world of sports, each and every day. Even on Christmas, some poor team is playing a game or a match somewhere. And you can be sure a whole bunch of sad-sack gamblers is ducking out of Christmas dinner to check on the score.

At this point, you might be asking—what about Atlantic City and Las Vegas? How come legal gambling establishments haven't driven wiseguys out of the gaming business? The reason, once again, has to do with the deviant nature of gamblers themselves. Sure, it is nice to go to Atlantic City and take in a show and have a fine dinner and then play the slots or maybe some roulette or even a little poker. What's more, it's perfectly legal and even encouraged by politicians and tourist boards. But there is a catch, and a pretty big one—you got to pay taxes on whatever you win. After all, when you gamble in an Atlantic City casino, you are involved in a legitimate business transaction that is fully subject to state and federal tax laws. And the casino will have a record of the number of chips you cashed in and the amount of money you walked out with. A copy of that record will be forwarded to old Uncle Sam.

That is simply too much paperwork to please the average degenerate gambler. You see, these sicko gamblers, in their warped and twisted minds, always believe that the next hand they play, the next game they bet on, will be the Big Score, and none of them want to pay taxes on the Big Score. I mean, they are absolutely convinced that the next bet will pay off and pay off big, even if they are on a ten-game losing streak—*especially* if they are on a ten-game losing streak. Doesn't matter what the odds are or who is playing or what factors affect the outcome—it is simply the foundation of a gambler's belief system that the Big Score is always one bet away. That is what keeps them going, what excites them to their very cores. This naïve, foolish belief in "being overdue" is a gambler's biggest flaw—and, as a result, the thing that wiseguys exploit most readily. In a casino, all winnings are reported to the government and thus taxable at a very high rate. But when you bet with the Mafia, it is just you and your bookie—no official record, no eye in the sky, no nothing. And you keep one hundred percent of your winnings.

As a result, gambling will always be a big-bucks business for the mob. The real beauty of gambling as an operation, though, is that the overhead is extremely low. The absolute lowest guy in the pecking order can be used as a bookmaker. It can be an associate or someone with even less ties to the family. The training is minimal, and the operation can be run out of a guy's bedroom. You don't have to pull a mask over your head and stick a gun in somebody's ear; you just sit back and wait for the money to be handed over. Wiseguys like making money any way they can, but they absolutely love making money with a minimal expenditure of energy. And gambling produces wads of money with no greater effort than picking up the phone.

The agent through which all this money passes from gambler to gangster is the bookie. A bookie needs to establish himself in his neighborhood as the man to see if you want to place a bet. This is not all that hard to do. Word gets around and over time you earn a reputation. Some bookies set themselves up on the same street corner everyday, so gamblers know where to go to find them. Others handle most if not all of their bets over the phone. Some bookie operations are very low-tech—just one guy and one phone. Other operations are more sophisticated—a bank of phones in a rented office and maybe even a wire room, feeding fresh odds to bookies round the clock. Lefty, my Mafia mentor, was a bookie. He ran the bookmaking operation for the underboss of the Bonanno crime family, Nicky Marangello. The whole thing was run over a single phone set up in the back of Lefty's social club in Little Italy. One of the ways I ingratiated myself with Lefty was by placing fifty- and hundred-dollar bets with him on baseball, football and the ponies.

Lefty was a bright guy, but you don't need to have all that much on the ball to be a bookie. You can't be a total screwup, but you don't need to be a rocket scientist, either. Basically, all you have to do is know the odds to all the games you take action on and keep good records on who bet what. If the sport that you are handling is football or basketball, you can get the odds right out of the *New York Post*. If it's baseball or hockey, you might have to get the line from a sports book in Las Vegas. Either way, no big deal. Another thing you have to do is figure out how much action to accept from different gamblers. A mob bookie takes all sorts of bets, from a single dollar to a nickel (five hundred dollars) to a dime (one thousand dollars) to ten or fifteen grand and, on rare occasions, even more. It all depends on the gambler. You have to know what he can reasonably be expected to pay should he lose, what amount will not break him and terminate his business with you. For the most part, bookies take bets of around a grand or two on games, and allow the more hard-core gamblers among their clientele to bet around ten grand a week. None of this money changes hands the day of the actual bet. A bookie allows his clients to run up a tab of losses. At the end of a week, the client has to settle up and pay the difference between what he has won and what he has lost. Once in a while, it will be the bookie paying out to an unusually lucky client. But in the vast majority of weeks, it is the bookie collecting money from the gambler. A bookie beats you far, far more than you beat a bookie. Just like in Las Vegas and Atlantic City, the advantage is always with the house.

Most of the action will be on college and pro-football games. Gamblers really get pumped up for a good football game. Plenty of action, also, on basketball and the horses. Few things in sports are as thrilling as the couple of minutes it takes for a thoroughbred race-horse to thunder his way to victory—especially if you've got a few bucks on the outcome. Bookies also take numbers. Here you have people trying to pick three numbers and winning something like six hundred dollars for a one-dollar bet if they get them right. The Italian lottery, some people call it. The numbers, generally, are the last three digits in the published daily take from a particular race-track. You just open up the *Daily News*, see what yesterday's total track haul was at Aqueduct or the Meadowlands, and take the last three digits—they are that day's "number." Those numbers are selected because they are generally thought to be unfixable. Some bookies get subordinates or even young kids to run numbers for them—that is, run around the neighborhood scooping up numbers bets from different people.

But the most important thing a bookie does is collect his winnings. His most essential skill is extracting money from gamblers who generally don't have any and certainly don't want to part with the little they have. There is no mystery to how he does this. It is all based on the simple premise that if you don't pay your bookie, your bookie will throw you a beating. If you lose a bunch of bets in a row and miss a couple of payments, okay, maybe your bookie gives you a stern and threatening warning. But if you keep falling deeper and deeper into that hole, you stand a very good chance of getting a leg snapped in two. Like everything else in the Mafia, bookmaking runs on intimidation and fear. Gamblers know full well what they are getting into, and they are willing to roll the dice. That they would rather take the chance of bodily harm than pay taxes on potential winnings is just another example of the twisted pathology of the degenerate gambler. But, hey, it is not for wiseguys to clue-in these numbskulls to the folly of their ways. They are here to fully exploit that weakness until all that is left is the hollow husk of what was once a human being. Now, wiseguys don't really want to kill the goose that lays the golden egg. They want to keep their gamblers healthy and happy, so they keep betting and losing and paying up. But they will throw a beating if the gambler starts getting sloppy with payments. And if you become a total fucking deadbeat, wiseguys will whack you and eat the loss. Wiseguys want their gamblers to be degenerate—but not too degenerate. Once you become a giant headache, it is easier for wiseguys to just cut their losses.

Which brings us to another mob endeavor that is inexorably linked to gambling—the time-honored practice of loan-sharking. Oftentimes, wiseguys will get convicted of both gambling and loan-sharking at once. Frank D'Amato, a New Jersey wiseguy, recently got ten years on conspiracy charges for loan-sharking and gambling. Put simply, loan-sharking is the activity of lending money at an exorbitant rate of interest. That interest—called the "vigorish," or "vig"— is not computed monthly, as with most loans. It compounds every single week. Many degenerate gamblers wind up with no option but to turn to a Mafia loan shark—better known as a shylock—to secure the cash they need to pay off gambling debts. The thinking, once again, is that the high interest rate is not a problem, since they will be paying the whole thing off just as soon as they hit their next Big

Score. Which, as we now know, will happen any minute. This is what I mean by digging a deeper and deeper hole. Gamblers end up owing thousands to their bookie and thousands more to their shylock. Eventually, their gambling debts grow so big that they are cut off from making any more bets, eliminating the chance that they can make enough money to satisfy their shylocks. Now they have to find another bookie in another part of town. Maybe they even go and find another shylock, too. Now they have debts all over the place. This, my friends, is an extremely dangerous way to conduct business. You are flirting with all sorts of evil shit if you string along a bunch of bookies and shylocks for too long. Eventually, the whole thing is going to collapse. And your broken body will wind up buried beneath it all.

And yet, as clear as the hazards of taking out a loan with a shylock may be, this does not seem to stop too many people from doing it. The appeal, of course, is that there are no forms to fill out, no credit checks to endure. You walk up to a shylock, you walk away with the cash you need. What's more, there are a variety of options when it comes to taking out a loan. Here is how they work.

Say you borrow ten grand from a shy. The shy will tell you what the vig is on the loan. Ordinarily, the vig on a ten-grand loan will be either three or five points, with each point representing one hundred dollars. Remember, the vig is payable every week, so five points means five hundred dollars a week in interest. First week passes, you've got to find your shy and pay at least the vig to keep him happy. Now, maybe you had a good week at the track and you have an extra five grand that you want to use to pay down the principal of your loan. Sorry, but no can do. You are not allowed to pay down the loan in increments. If you want to settle it, you have to pay the whole amount at once. This ain't a bank, after all, and shylocks aren't interested in partial payments and all that crap. If you want to terminate that ten-grand loan, you got to pay off the ten grand plus the vig that first week. If you don't have it, then you just pay the vig. Those are your only options. If you're not careful, you can wind up paying many times the amount of your loan in interest. Happens all the time. And we all know what happens if you miss a couple of vig payments in a row.

That is why the wiseguy term for these loans is "blood money." Blood money is any loan that will cause blood to be extracted if not promptly paid back. Sometimes the blood will be extracted after a single missed payment of non-principal-reducing interest. Someone desperate for cash can also opt to get their hands on what is known as "fast money." Fast money is a short-term loan, payable in full after a predetermined period. Sometimes it is called a "five for nine" deal, which means a guy borrows five hundred dollars on Monday and must repay nine hundred dollars by Friday.

There is also something called a "Chinese loan," which means you've got a longer period of time to pay the exorbitant interest. Maybe the shylock gives you a full thirty days to pay the vig, as opposed to the standard seven days. Worst of all, however, is the dreaded "knockdown loan." When you are foolish enough to take out one of these, you should be advised not to miss a single vig payment. If you do miss one, the missed interest payment is added to the principal. Now you owe the vig that you missed, and a much higher loan amount. Miss another one, and it gets added on again. That, if you haven't already figured out, can get pretty expensive. But don't worry if you can't make that first interest payment. You can always take out a Chinese loan to pay off the preexisting knockdown loan. That is, if you can find another bookie who doesn't know you're half a deadbeat.

Now, if you think wiseguys know enough not to mess around with gambling and shylocking, you're wrong. Plenty of wiseguys gamble, and plenty take out loans from shylocks. Gambling, in particular, is a big part of the wiseguy lifestyle. It fits in perfectly with their desire to make as much money with as little effort as humanly possible. Wiseguys have a lot of time to follow sporting events, juggle spreads, go to the track, all of that. Lefty, Sonny, all of those guys bet all the time. Lefty, in particular, was a degenerate gambler. This guy loved to bet on the horses, and he routinely lost thousands of dollars—one time, ten thousand—in a day. He would bet his last dollar on a race, even though he knew very little about horses and was not good at handicapping them. Lefty was always saddled with huge gambling debts. At one point he told me he owed Nicky Marangello $160,000. It got so bad, he couldn't even get made until he squared up one of his gambling debts. He finally did and got his button in 1977. Didn't stop him from gambling, though. The whole time I knew him, Lefty was basically flat broke from all the money he threw away at the track.

Generally, it is fine for wiseguys to gamble, as long as they don't become total degenerates. If a wiseguy's gambling habit starts to spin out of control, he will be called in by the family for a sit-down and told to clean up his act, or else. If he doesn't heed this useful advice and continues to bottom out, he could very well get himself whacked. What good is a wiseguy to his captain if he cannot be trusted not to squander money on long shot bets?

Even so, wiseguys will bet on anything—and do anything to win. Sonny Black used to like to arm-wrestle me, but I always won and pretty easily at that. This guy could not stand losing over and over again. Finally, he calls me over and tells me that today is the day he beats me at arm wrestling. We get our elbows in place, and Sonny says, "Go." Then he spits right in my face. I am startled, and Sonny slams my hand to the table. Victory is his at last.

The moral of the story is this: If you're going to gamble with wiseguys, you better know the odds are stacked against you. Every fucking time.

6

WISEGUYS AND WOMEN

This guy I knew, let's call him Patsy, funny as hell and a good storyteller. Patsy went around six-foot-four and 230 pounds. He liked to come in and tell us about the broads he fucked.

So he tells us about this one broad he was out with this one night. Says the woman asked him, "Hey, Patsy, you into kinky sex?" Patsy says, yeah, why not, even though he's not into anything kinky. Most mobsters are pretty conventional when it comes to sex. But if the broad asks you, you say, sure, why not, what you got in mind? The broad says, "I like to get slapped around a bit. How about hitting me?"

So Patsy gives her a little rap on the chops, nothing major. The broad says, "Patsy, come on, you got to hit me harder." Patsy obliges.

"I hauled back and I fucking punched her and knocked her the fuck out," he told us. "After a while, the broad comes around and says, 'Hey, Patsy, next time? Not so hard.'"

Patsy's over-enthusiastic foreplay notwithstanding, wiseguys tend to be respectful of and gentlemanly towards the women in their lives. They can be cruel and sadistic scumbags to fellow wiseguys and other men, but with women they are as courteous as the average guy, and maybe even a little more so.

Start with mom: wiseguys love their mothers to death. Making a crack about another wiseguy's mother is an offense that might get you whacked. Even the most brutal wiseguy will be a teddy bear in the presence of the woman who raised him. Remember the scene in *Goodfellas* where, right after whacking someone, DeNiro and Pesci go get a knife at Pesci's mother's house and end up having dinner with her? These two ruthless, remorseless killers are absolute pussycats around this tiny, saintly woman. Hang around wiseguys, and you will find that scene is very true to life. Next to the boss of their mob family, there is no one to whom a wiseguy shows more deference than dear, sweet mom.

Then there is the wife. Believe it or not, wiseguys also treat their wives with decency and respect. That might seem like a ridiculous statement, considering that nine out of ten wiseguys have a girlfriend on the side. But fooling around comes with the lifestyle—we'll get to that in a minute. Whatever they do when they are at the club or out on the town, wiseguys make fairly decent husbands when they are at home.

For instance, wiseguys rarely curse in front of their wives. It is unusual to hear a wiseguy use profanity in the presence of any woman. Sure, you'll see mobsters on TV shows curse at their wives and so forth. But in all my years in the mob, I never once saw a wiseguy get a dirty mouth around a woman. Whores, of course, don't count.

Wiseguys also take pretty good care of their wives and their families. They are excellent providers. You will meet very few mobsters who are deadbeat dads or husbands. Father of the year, they ain't, but a wiseguy who allows his family situation to spiral out of control will not be viewed kindly by his superiors in the mob. You must keep things running as smoothly as you can on the family front, and that usually means keeping the wife happy any way you can. For some wives, that means having your husband home for dinner every night. Other wives simply need wads of cash to stay in line. Whatever it takes, you do it. Wiseguys have enough strife and stress on the job—they don't need a lot of headaches waiting for them at home.

That said, wiseguys are not immune from the usual problems that confront ordinary married couples. No matter how hard you try to keep everyone happy at home, you will inevitably have problems that you have to deal with as the man of the house. Wiseguys have overdue bills to pay, wives that nag the shit out of them, kids that dabble in drugs and flunk out of school, mothers-in-law who are a giant pain in the ass. Usually, the wife will handle things like going to parent-teacher meetings and taking the kids to the doctor. But the pressures are there for a wiseguy nonetheless. It's kind of funny, actually, that these guys who flout many of society's conventions and live largely lawless lives and kill other human beings without batting an eye are, when it comes to marriage and family, pretty much like you and me. Squabbles over dinner, arguments about spending, fights with the kids, indifferent sex—in the few hours that a wiseguy spends at home every day, his life is fairly indistinguishable from the unhappily married fuck who lives next door.

Most of the mobsters I knew, however, genuinely loved their wives. Certainly Lefty did: he was always sweet and tender to her when I was around. Spend a day with him, and you might think he didn't have a tender bone in his body, but around his wife he was, indeed, a gentleman. Of course, loving your wife does not preclude keeping a girlfriend on the side, at least not in the world of the wiseguy.

If you look at it objectively, a wiseguy's extramarital activity hardly sets him apart from the common man; if anything, it makes him seem like an average Joe. All sorts of married people are out there having affairs. What is it, five out of every ten marriages that end in divorce? Based on that statistic, it's not much of a stretch to guess that at least five out of every ten married guys have a girlfriend stashed away somewhere.

With wiseguys, maybe that number goes up to eight or nine out of ten. The typical married mobster has at least one girlfriend on the side. The fact is that the wiseguy lifestyle lends itself to being unfaithful. There are tons of available women hanging around all the time, the type of women who are attracted to wiseguys. Those types of women tend to be aggressive and available. What's more, wiseguys spend a lot more time socializing than normal people. Most people sow their oats in their twenties and thirties, get married, and then more or less settle down. Certainly they aren't going out every night when they are in their forties and fifties. But wiseguys go bouncing pretty much six out of seven nights a week. They have dinner at home with their families, tuck their kids into bed, kiss their wives, and go out for *four or five more hours*. They go to hot nightclubs, fancy restaurants, discos, bars, you name it. Think about the temptation you would face if you spent several hours out on the town surrounded by pretty women almost every fucking night. It is basically a fact of the wiseguy lifestyle that you succumb to these temptations and find yourself a *gumata* so that you can then go home and keep things fairly calm and orderly in your household.

Some wiseguys will set their girlfriends up with an apartment and a stipend, so that they always have a place to meet them. Others will not spring for their *gumata's* rent. Depends on how fucking cheap you are. Some wiseguys are fine with just one girlfriend, others will keep two or three. Also a matter of choice. Some will take their girlfriends out on the town and introduce them to the guys; others will not be seen with them in public. What surprised me when I hung out with wiseguys was how often they preferred spending the night bullshitting with each other to spending it with their girlfriends. Sometimes visiting the girlfriend almost became an obligation, just like going home to the wife. Wiseguys are most comfortable, most in their element, when they are hanging out with each other, talking sports, planning scores, shooting the shit. Ideally, the girlfriend is squeezed in later in the evening, and only for an hour, maybe two.

Most, if not all, wiseguy wives know full well what is going on behind their backs. As long as a wiseguy is suitably discrete and doesn't do something stupid like fuck his wife's best friend or the lady who cleans the house, then he can spend a couple of hours with his *gumata* here and there with no consequences. A wiseguy wife knows not to ask her husband about his business or how he spent his day, and therefore there is no way for her to find out if he is having an affair. Just as a wiseguy wife doesn't want to know too much about who her husband may have whacked that day, there is no point in spending too much time worrying about who your husband may or may not be fucking. It is simply one of the many privileges of being a wiseguy, and women who are drawn to and marry wiseguys know this all too well. As long as you don't get sloppy in your activity and behave disrespectfully to your wife, things should work out swell.

Of course, girlfriends can be a whole other source of stress and pressure for wiseguys. Instead of just one woman busting your balls, now you have two or maybe three. Instead of one woman's set of problems to hear about and deal with, now you have twice as many irritations and insecurities in your life. Sure, a wiseguy can dump his girlfriend and find another who will allow him at least a few weeks of fun before jumping on him for being late or not spending Saturdays with her or forgetting her birthday. But, inevitably, there will be grief—that sort of comes with the territory, too.

All in all, though, it's a pretty good deal for the wiseguy. And who's to say it's wrong? I can tell you this—a lot fewer than five out of ten wiseguys get divorced.

7

WISEGUY TABLE MANNERS

We were down in Florida in a pretty ritzy French restaurant—me, three wiseguys, and three female companions. The lighting in this place was so low it was practically pitch dark, and the stuck-up French waiter had to come around with a little penlight so you could read the fucking menu.

So this waiter is walking around with his little flashlight, and nobody can read their menu until he comes over. Naturally, the waiter attends to the females first. He's fussing all over them with his little penlight, describing dishes and helping them pick out entrees and all that bullshit. The rest of us are sitting around trying to read the fucking menus in the dark.

Finally, one of the wiseguys says, "I can't see a fucking thing; this is fucking ridiculous." So he reaches over and grabs the waiter by the arm and yanks him away from one of the ladies. He grabs the guy's hand, points the flashlight on his menu and starts ordering before any of the broads get a chance. Ladies first? Not in the world of the wiseguy.

HOW TO EMBARRASS
A WISEGUY

Want to know how to embarrass a wiseguy? You can't. There's no way. It is impossible to embarrass a wiseguy. Wiseguys have no shame.

For some reason, that's one of the defining traits of a wiseguy. They feel they are always in the right, no matter what they're doing. If it's distasteful to other people, then the other people are wrong. A gangster's way of life is always the right way; the joke is on everybody else. That's why you always see wiseguys walk into a place like they own it. They have absolutely no shame—they are maybe the least self-conscious people you'll ever encounter.

Uncomfortable situations that would embarrass normal people, wiseguys simply shrug off. One time, in the middle of a shooting war, we all had to walk around carrying our guns. Personally, the only time I carried a gun is when a wiseguy gave me one to carry. And the only time they did was when there was a shooting war going on. And I'm not talking about those new, shiny guns you see in movies and on TV. Mobsters work with these rusty old piece-of-shit guns they get from God knows where. In the movies, you always see wiseguys pulling guns out of holsters. Nobody walks around with their gun in a holster, either. No shoulder holsters, no ankle holsters—I never seen anybody carry a gun in a holster, at least not a wiseguy. Wiseguys carry their guns in their pockets or tucked into their belts.

Anyway, we had this one guy, we called him Jimmy Legs. Jimmy was about six-foot-five and skinny, except for his big fucking belly. Jimmy carried this beat-up old .45 caliber gun that he liked to tuck under his belt. Problem was his enormous belly. Imagine trying to tie a belt around an egg. Jimmy wore his pants about a mile below his stomach, and his gun kept slipping off his waist and falling out through his pant leg. Michael Corleone, this guy wasn't.

Jimmy had to come up with something, and what he came up with was an extra pocket. He had his wife sew a pocket onto the back of his pants, just above his ass. He comes in and shows all the guys how he carries his gun tucked away in this extra pocket. Brilliant idea, he says. We consider it for a moment, then we shrug.

The extra pocket works fine until a couple of days later, when Jimmy comes into the club and says he's not feeling too well. Says he's got a bad case of the runs. Every ten minutes he's rushing to the john, back and forth. About the fifth time he's in there we hear him laughing like crazy. What the hell is this guy laughing at? He's in there shitting his pants—what's funny about that? Finally Jimmy comes out and he's holding his gun between his thumb and index finger, like it's infected or something. Turns out it is. Jimmy tells us how he forget he had his gun in his extra pocket, and when he ran into the toilet, his gun fell in the bowl and got shit all over it. So he's laughing and saying how from now on, he doesn't have to worry about his aim when he shoots at people. All he has to do is nick them and they'll die of toxic poisoning from his shitty gun.

Embarrassed? Not for a second. Like I said, you cannot embarrass a wiseguy. Go ahead, try sometime. Better yet, take my word for it.

9

WISEGUYS DON'T LIKE TO WAIT

Me and Tony Mirra are in a mall trying to find a pay phone. Tony Mirra, you have to realize, is one of the meanest guys I ever met and a real asshole by anyone's standards. A total fucking jerk who even other wiseguys don't like. He was a big guy, six-foot-two and maybe 220 pounds, and he had a big mouth to match. When I was out with him, I always expected something bad to happen.

Me and Tony walk around this mall and finally we find a pay phone. Problem is, some lady is using it. She's this mousy little housewife with her mousy little husband standing next to her, watching their two little kids. You can tell they're from out of town, from Indiana or Illinois or who the fuck knows where. Me, I'm okay waiting, but Tony wants to use the phone and he wants to use it now.

So we wait fifteen, twenty seconds, and finally Tony says, "When are you going to be off the fucking phone?"

The lady is shocked. She says something like, "I don't know. I'm talking, in a minute."

Tony says, "Well, you been on that fucking phone long enough."

The poor husband is standing right there, and he doesn't do a thing. You can tell he is totally intimidated and embarrassed.

Tony says, "I need to use the fucking phone, so get off the phone, you fucking cunt."

I say, "Tony, for Christ's sake, leave the lady alone, you're embarrassing her husband, and you're scaring her kids."

He says, "I don't give a fuck, I need to use the fucking phone."

Then he turns to the poor housewife and says, "Now hang up the fucking phone, you bitch."

Finally, the lady hangs up and this nice little family slinks away, shaken and terrified. The husband has been emasculated right in front of his wife. I feel pretty bad his kids had to see it.

Tony Mirra makes his call like nothing happened.

10

WHY WISEGUYS
NEVER LOSE FIGHTS

When you grow up on the streets, you get into a lot of street fights. No way around it, plain and simple. That's why a lot of your champion boxers grew up on the streets. In Paterson, New Jersey, I got into situations all the time where the only way out was with my fists. The first time you punch someone in the face, you are almost shocked by the violence of it, the blood, the crunching sound, the breaking bones. After that, it's a piece of cake. I punched a lot of people in my day, almost always in situations where it was punch or be punched.

One thing I knew to not do was go looking for a street fight. Why provoke a fight when the guy might have a knife or a gun? If, however, you sense that a fight is inevitable, you must make sure you get in the first punch. Once I started hanging out with wiseguys, though, I was surprised at how they went around almost eager to mix it up. They knew they had a tremendous advantage over almost everyone who crossed their paths: an utter fearlessness about fighting. Wiseguys do everything with their fists: fighting is a way to negotiate, send a message, settle a debt, even have a little fun on a slow night. I saw wiseguys beat up waiters, shopkeepers, cab drivers, you name it. And I never saw a wiseguy lose a fight. If you ever have the misfortune to be punched by a wiseguy, you will not soon forget it. I got punched by wiseguys a couple of times. They punch pretty good.

Of course, I was a federal agent, so I couldn't go around looking for people to beat up. There were times as Donnie Brasco when I had no choice but to join in when the wiseguys decided to throw someone a beating. A couple of times I even instigated a fight myself, but only to keep my cover from being blown. And there were a couple of instances where I stepped in and gave someone a beating, to spare him from getting pummeled by a real wiseguy.

In the wiseguy world, fights happen all the time, out of the blue. Even after I gave up my identity as Donnie Brasco, I did not lose my instinct for fighting. One time, some agents pulled me in to help them with another undercover job. This one was overseas, and I was supposed to play a big-time New York wiseguy. We went out to dinner one night, me and the other agents, in a restaurant where we were probably the only Americans. Sure enough, these four guys in there, I guess they had too much to drink, but they start talking a lot of shit about America in their broken English. Obviously they are trying to get our goats. We let it go, just blow it off, because the last thing we want to do is get into some problem situation in this foreign country where we don't even speak the language. But these guys don't let up. They keep bashing Americans and trying to provoke us and they keep getting louder and louder. Finally, one of these drunken guys gets up and comes to our table.

This guy stands next to where I'm sitting down and keeps up his tirade about us ugly Americans. I say, "Look, fella, why don't you just go away and don't bother us, we don't want any trouble." Then a second guy comes over and the two of them are sort of hovering over us, going on and on about Americans. This time I say, "Look, you're a little too close to me, so move the fuck away." But no, these guys keep mouthing off and moving even closer to me. Finally I say, "If you don't step back I'm going to lay you out right here where you stand."

Now, already I have violated the first rule of street fighting: punch first, talk later. Here I am negotiating with these menacing drunks. Had this happened to real wiseguys, these drunks would have been swallowing teeth long before they came over to our table. But I'm a government agent undercover in a foreign country. For me to get into a big bar fight and get hauled off by police would be a giant hassle, or maybe even an international incident. So I try to talk my way out of the situation. Deep down, I know it's not going to work.

Just as I tell one guy I am going to lay him out, I see the other guy start coming at me. He was a little behind me, so he gets a pretty good jump on me, but before he can sucker punch me, my fellow agent gets up and hits the guy in the face, knocks him flat. I get up and hit the other guy, and he goes down, too. Two punches, fight's over. Me and the other agent, we calmly put some money on the table and walk out of the joint. No need to stick around and wait for cops.

Now, these drunken bums got lucky in a way they'll never understand. Had I been a real wiseguy, the punches would not have stopped at one. They would have been beaten to bloody pulps, maybe to death. I have seen wiseguys beat the hell out of people. It takes a while to do, could take a couple of dozen punches, but if you know where and how to punch a guy, believe me, you can kill him. What those guys did to us—talk trash, try to intimidate us—was more than enough to earn them the beating of their lives. Hell, people have been savagely beaten for accidentally bumping into wiseguys.

So, if you get into some kind of altercation with someone who looks like a wiseguy, walk away. No, run away. Wiseguys love getting into fights, and they never lose.

11

WISEGUYS DON'T
MAKE RESERVATIONS

Say you're out for a night on the town with your friends, your coworkers, your family. You walk into one of the best restaurants in the city, the place everyone wants to try. You can smell the steaks grilling in the kitchen, see the glamorous people laughing and drinking—you know this is going to be one of those special nights. You walk up to the maître d', and you give him your name.

And the maître d' says, "Sorry, you have no reservation."

Whoops. What happens now? Maybe you made a reservation, and the hostess forgot to put it in the book. Maybe your secretary forgot to call and make one. Maybe you yourself forgot to call ahead. The point is, here you are, surrounded by friends and family, and your special night is about to go down the toilet. What do you do? What can you do?

Here's what ninety-nine percent of the population would do—they would turn right around and leave.

Now, here's what wiseguys would do.

The maître d' tells them they have no reservation and thus no table. Well, that will hardly be a surprise to the wiseguys. Wiseguys never ever make restaurant reservations. They just show up at some five-star joint and give the maître d' some made-up name. When no reservation is found, that's when wiseguys do their wiseguy thing.

I remember going to one fancy place in lower Manhattan with Sonny Black and Lefty Ruggiero and a few other guys, and the host telling us there was no reservation in our name. The place is packed, bustling, but what did we care? "What do you mean, no reservation?" Lefty demanded, his voice rising above the clatter of the restaurant. "Check again." Then Sonny piped up, nice and loudly, and then I said something, and then pretty soon all of us were angry and yelling and making a fuss, and all the nice patrons were looking up from their linguini and staring our way. The maître d' looked like he wanted to crawl inside the dumbwaiter. We not only kept up our racket, but we got even louder and acted more insulted. "No table? How can there be no fucking table? Check the fucking book again."

Within minutes, we had the best table in the house.

How'd we do it? Did they make room for us—which restaurants can always do—because they knew we were wiseguys? Well, certainly we didn't look like broom salesmen from Boise. But, more importantly, they satisfied our demand, however irrational it was, simply to get us to stop making a fuss. Most people don't like fusses. The managers of stuffy restaurants *hate* fusses.

And so they figured out a way to accommodate us. The fact is, most people don't have the stomach for confrontation that wiseguys have. Wiseguys are absolutely unafraid to confront people, even if they know they are dead wrong about something. For wiseguys, a wrong can be turned into a right simply by arguing your point loudly and forcibly. The value of getting in someone's face and knocking them off-balance cannot be overstated. Wiseguys know this— wiseguys understand the currency of fear.

Now, truth be told, sometimes wiseguys don't even have to make a fuss to get their way. Our reputations precede us almost everywhere we go. One time, as Donnie Brasco, I accompanied some wiseguys to Milwaukee for a meeting with Frank Balistrieri, boss of Milwaukee's top crime family. When we got there, there was a big dinner scheduled at a local hotel, something called an icebreaker. Lots of big wigs, politicians, union people, the works. Well, at the last minute, Balistrieri decides that he wants to attend the icebreaker. There are probably ten of us in the group, and of course we have made no arrangements to attend this sit-down dinner. So we show up at this elegant affair and go right into the dining room and approach the maître d'. It is obvious that there isn't a free table in the place—it's packed. Nevertheless, we show up and start talking about how hungry we are. There is no question in any of our minds that we will soon be eating.

Sure enough, the maître d' takes one look at us and springs into action. Surely, he recognizes Balistrieri. We see the maître d' scurry across the restaurant and go up to this table where a group of diners are already digging into their salads. There is some discussion and a lot of puzzled looks, but before long, these poor bastards are all getting up from the table and being wedged into other tables, one here, two there, that sort of thing. Some busboys whip the table into shape, and within minutes we are seated.

It was obvious that the maître d' was absolutely shitting his pants. No way was he going to tell us he couldn't accommodate us. He made sure we not only got a table, but that we go one of the best tables in the place. And we sat there as if it was our due.

Which, in a way, it was. You see, you pretty much get what you ask for in this life, and most people are too timid to ask for what they want. And getting what you want out of life—isn't that the whole game? Most people have no idea how this game is played.

But wiseguys do.

Now, nobody is saying that you should walk into a restaurant and bully the maître d' and make a pig out of yourself and basically threaten someone into giving you a table. But walking out of the restaurant with your tail between your legs isn't the way to go, either. You can usually get what you want by being direct, forceful, and unrelenting—you'll find most people wither in the face of such resolve.

Realize that confrontation is not always a bad thing, and you'll get more out of life. And we're not just talking about a good corner table.

12

WISEGUYS WON'T
BE IGNORED

I'm down in Miami with a bunch of wiseguys at this fancy nightclub. Not surprisingly, they sit us in the front row, at a big table right below the stage. A comedian is working the joint, and we're laughing and having a good time until the comic starts making wisecracks about our table.

Obviously, the guy recognizes us as wiseguys and can't resist making references to these Mafia hoods. Cracks about how we look, what we're eating, who we're going to beat up, all that. The crowd is eating it up. The guy's on a roll with the mob jokes and shows no sign of stopping.

Finally my boss leans over to me and says, "Donnie, get up there and tell him to lay off this table."

I say, "The guy's on stage. You want me to go up there in front of everybody?"

My guy says, "I don't care where he is. Just go up and tell him to direct his comments to another table."

So I get up and walk right on stage and go up to the comic and whisper in his ear, "Listen, I think you better move on to other material and don't make any more wisecracks about our table." Everybody's watching this, wondering what the fuck is going on. The guy nods; I sit back down; the show goes on.

And the comic keeps making jokes about our table.

Evidently, the guy doesn't get it. My boss leans over and says, "Get back up there and tell him again." So I go up and tell him again to move along, pick another table.

"Do not make any more cracks about us," I say. This time, the guy listens and starts telling jokes about something else. But before long, he's back to us, cracking wise about the mobsters in the front row.

My boss doesn't tell me to go back up there, and I know what that means. It means wait until the show is over to deliver the message. The comic's set ends, and he bounds off the stage, and me and another wiseguy follow him to his dressing room. I grab the guy's elbow and he looks at me like a startled deer.

I get up close and tell him, "Look, when someone tells you to do something, you got to learn to do it. Because, otherwise, it will be dangerous to your health." Believe it or not, the guy *still* doesn't get it. Instead of apologizing, he starts mouthing off: Can't you take a joke, what's the big deal, this is how I do my act, and I'm not changing for anyone. Now, I have no choice. I punch him in the stomach, nice and hard. There is nothing like the sight of a man doubled over in pain and making gurgling sounds to let you know your message is finally getting through.

Look, I always tried everything I could not to have to rough people up, but lots of times I had no choice but to work someone over. I always told myself that the guy was actually lucky, because if some real mobster got the job instead of me, he'd get a much worse ass kicking from a guy who enjoyed every minute of it. I also understood that violence is the glue that holds a wiseguy's way of life together. Regular people have several options when it comes to getting their messages across. They can write a letter or hire a lawyer or take out a fucking ad. Wiseguys don't go for polite persuasion. Fear and intimidation are their only strategies. This stupid comic, he finally got the message. And the message was: when a wiseguy tells you to do something, it ain't a comedy bit. It's for real.

13

WISEGUYS DON'T HIDE WHO THEY ARE

Wiseguys are not hard to pick out of a crowd. Not because of how they dress or the way they style their hair, though those things help. You can spot a wiseguy a block away from the way he walks. Call it the wiseguy strut.

Wiseguys have this easy shuffle to their walk, a slow, confident swing to their gait. They walk around like they own the streets, which, in effect, they do. That's because wiseguys do not hide the fact that they are wiseguys. They do not disguise themselves or slink around or otherwise try to blend in. Sure, they pretend to have legitimate jobs and do any number of things to steer clear of the law. But in their neighborhoods, on their streets, wiseguys basically announce themselves as wiseguys. It is a badge of honor to be connected in their neighborhoods, and, as a result, they are respected and even admired by their neighbors. In the places where they live and hang out, everybody knows who they are and what they do. Not only do citizens know who the wiseguys are, they know which wiseguys have more power than other wiseguys. Whatever your place in the pecking order, though, being a wiseguy in a wiseguy neighborhood makes you something of a celebrity and allows you to command the total respect of everyone who lives there.

Ordinary people in wiseguy neighborhoods get something in exchange for showing mobsters this respect. Neighborhoods that are dominated by wiseguys are also considered to be under the protection of these wiseguys. There are far fewer robberies, rapes, or muggings in wiseguy neighborhoods than in even the safest precincts of the city. Old ladies walk around at night feeling completely safe. You would have to be one stupid burglar to come into a mobbed-up neighborhood and knock off the corner bar. The fact is that people simply do not come into these neighborhoods and commit crimes. There isn't a police force in the world that deters crime as well as the presence of wiseguys. And it's not like wiseguys have to do anything to create this sense of calm and well-being. They simply have to live there to chase all kinds of riffraff away. Wiseguys maintain law and order in their neighborhoods through intimidation—their reputations most certainly precede them wherever they go.

Once it is known that wiseguys live in a certain area—New York City's Little Italy, for instance, or the block in Ozone Park that was home to John Gotti—that area instantly becomes a safe haven in an otherwise crazy city. These areas have the feel of small, cozy towns, governed by benign and folksy leaders. Wiseguys stroll their streets tipping their hats to the elderly, shaking hands with shop-keepers, tussling the hair of boys playing stickball, doing everything but kissing babies. They are the top dogs on their streets, and they know it. They are the mayor, police chief, and comptroller all rolled into one. Remember John Gotti openly defying police instructions not to detonate fireworks and thrilling his neighbors with an annual Fourth of July fireworks blowout? Gotti could have cared less what the cops and mayor wanted. What he cared about was taking care of his own. Wiseguys do not come into neighborhoods and make those neighborhoods worse. You would be one sorry wiseguy if people were getting robbed or harassed right under your nose. Wiseguys take great pride in knowing that their streets are safe and clean and filled with happy citizens walking their dogs, pushing their kids, living their lives—and respecting the wiseguys.

This mutually beneficial relationship between laypeople and the mobsters that live among them is the reason it is so hard for law enforcement agencies to root out wiseguys. Catching mobsters requires lengthy surveillance and loads of street intelligence, and both of those are difficult to accomplish in areas that are friendly to wiseguys. If there is any police activity in a certain neighborhood, any extended surveillance by feds in parked cars or vans, the citizens of that neighborhood are going to know about it, and they are going to make sure the wiseguys know about it, too. They will tell you that a strange Chevy has been parked on a certain street for a couple of hours, or that some suspicious looking fellows have been buzzing around the neighborhood in recent days. This is all the information a wiseguy needs to tidy up his act and lay low and do whatever he has to do to keep clean. Conducting good surveillance in wiseguy neighborhoods is difficult, because all kinds of ordinary neighbors are acting as informers and keeping the wiseguys one step ahead of their pursuers.

That's another reason wiseguys don't slink around and try to hide the fact that they are wiseguys. The more people who know who they are and what they do, the safer they are in their own neighborhoods. The respect, admiration, and, yes, fear that they command from ordinary people create a wall of protection around them, allowing them to feel at ease on their streets and in their social clubs. They are the masters of all they survey, or at least of a couple of city blocks. That is why you should have no problem picking out a wiseguy— look for the wiseguy strut.

So, if you find yourself suddenly living in a neighborhood dominated by wiseguys, count your blessings. You might have to put up with the occasional blood-drenched mob war. But otherwise, the crime rate is going to plummet.

14

THE BOSS

Me and Lefty met up with a bunch of other wiseguys outside this Italian restaurant on Mulberry Street one summer night. And that is where we stayed for the next couple hours—outside the joint. We stood there, hands in our pockets, grumpy looks on our faces, and just sort of milled around. We were not there to enjoy ourselves or shoot the shit. We were there to show respect for—and make sure no harm came to—one particular man inside the restaurant.

Not just any man, mind you. This was the Boss.

It is a ritual that plays out time and time again—tough wiseguys acting like toadies in the presence of the boss. That night, I asked Lefty why we couldn't simply go inside and sit down? He let me know there was a lot I had to learn about the ins and outs of Mafia leadership. Who was I to pull up a chair alongside Carmine Galante, boss of the Bonanno family? Lilo, as Galante was known, "don't sit down with anybody except captains and above," Lefty explained. "He don't sit down with soldiers or below, like you or me. He doesn't have anybody around him except people he wants. You can't even talk to this guy."

The fact is, there are ordinary wiseguys and then there are the bosses. Two very different things. The Mafia employs a very rigid hierarchy, more rigid than most companies and even the U.S. government. The man at the top of the pyramid—the boss of the family—is as powerful and inaccessible as any CEO or even the president. The boss is the unquestioned leader, the supreme dictator, the final arbiter, the ultimate wiseguy. His word is final, his decisions non-negotiable, his authority absolute. Around him, the meanest, most ruthless killers tremble with fear. You cannot understand the way of the wiseguy unless you understand the particular mystique of the Mafia boss.

Indeed, most of the glamorous history of the mob revolves around its bosses. Quite a few of them are now the stuff of legend. One of the most famous bosses of all time, for instance, was Al Capone, the notorious gangster who ruled Chicago in the '20s and early '30s. Capone consolidated his authority by whacking seven members of the Irish-American O'Banion gang in the fabled St. Valentine's Day Massacre of 1929. His incredible power over the gangs and illegal trades of Chicago was broken only when the feds nabbed him on income tax charges in 1931. Still, the legacy of Al Capone remains significant to this day. He truly thought of himself as a shrewd entrepreneur who ran a sweeping and profitable empire, even if he was known more for his murderous heart than for his business acumen.

In the end, mob bosses are just that—bosses. They oversee a variety of business endeavors, supervise a big team of employees, and settle disputes with other enterprises. Most of the decisions they make are routine business decisions. If this sounds pretty boring, that's because it is. Traditionally, mob bosses have not been as colorful as Al Capone. What's interesting is the amount of power they have and the sway they hold over the rest of the wiseguys.

That, perhaps, is the single most essential quality of a Mafia boss—the ability to exert influence over his family of gangsters. Make no mistake, a mob boss's authority derives from one thing and one thing only: fear. A boss absolutely must have the ability to instill fear in his men, allowing him to govern through intimidation and the implied threat of dire consequences for those who dare challenge him. For that reason, a mob boss must be ruthless and have some pretty heavy shit under his belt. He must bring with him a reputation for savagery and a history of settling disputes by shedding blood. This is the only way that he is going to be able to command the respect of his captains and of the other bosses. Not every boss is liked or admired, but every boss is feared and sometimes loathed. Carmine Galante, for instance, was not particularly liked by many wiseguys in the Bonanno family. But he was known as a serious wiseguy who not only made his bones under the family's legendary boss Joe Bonanno but also served a hard twelve years in jail for dealing heroin. That explains why we were out there that night in front of that restaurant and why he was afforded total respect by all the wiseguys. That is, until he was murdered by his underlings in 1979—but we'll get to that.

The bottom line is that every boss had to start out as a regular fucking soldier. He had to go through the same shit every wiseguy does, making scores, making his moves, earning respect, all of that. And, along the way, he had to have developed a desire to become the boss. Rarely does a wiseguy stumble reluctantly into the top slot or come out of nowhere to get the job. A wiseguy has to want the position, want it very badly, and want it for quite a while. A wiseguy who wants to be the boss may have to stifle his ambitions for years and years while the existing boss plays out his run. Vacancies do not come up all that often, though these days they come up more and more. In old times, bosses were bosses for decades. Today, because of bad management decisions and aggressive federal prosecution, there is more turnover. Still, patience is a key virtue if you have your eyes on the ultimate prize.

So, how does a wiseguy go about becoming the boss? Couple different ways. The easiest, smoothest way is if the existing boss dies of natural causes. Then the wiseguy beneath him—the underboss—almost always ascends to the top spot. Unless, of course, his position as underboss is shaky. Perhaps there are some captains who feel the underboss is not the best guy to become boss. Perhaps he is seen as weak and irrelevant. In that case, there may be a challenge to his becoming the boss. There may even be a couple of different guys who want the job. In that sense, it is different from some big company where management decides between three or four candidates for the top job. What it all comes down to is power.

If a wiseguy wants to challenge the ascension of the underboss to boss, he, basically, must line up as many other captains as he can behind him. He must make it clear that the real power of the family is behind him and not behind the underboss. There are a lot of politics involved. You will see a captain going around to different social clubs, holding secret meetings with captains, making his pitch to them, and trying to line up their support. For sure, he is going to have to convince some captains who support the underboss to switch their allegiance to him. After a while, the smoke clears, and it becomes apparent who holds the most influence over the rest of the family—the underboss or the challenging captain. When that happens, the one with the most power is essentially elected boss of the family, even though there might not be an actual vote.

Filling in for a boss who died naturally is one way to get the job. Another is to wait for the boss to end up in prison. Most bosses who get sent to jail for long stretches decide to step aside and allow someone else to become boss of the family. You get five to ten, maybe you remain the boss. But you get a hundred years, what are you going to do? It is simply a matter of convenience and common sense. Still, plenty of bosses refuse to step aside, even when they are in the slammer for years and years. Most likely, these are bosses who clawed their way to power and aren't likely to let go of the brass ring under any circumstances.

Then there is the most decisive and despicable way to the top—by whacking the boss. Now, in theory, this is not supposed to happen all that often. Wiseguys are not supposed to go around whacking bosses on a whim. In fact, the Mafia Commission, which includes representatives from all the area's families, is supposed to have a say in whether or not a boss can be whacked. Maybe a captain has consolidated a nice little power base for himself and goes in front of the Commission and argues his case that the existing boss is losing his effectiveness or does not have the family's best interests at heart. If the Commission deems a change in leadership appropriate, they will approve the assassination. If, however, they feel that whacking the boss will create a mess and disrupt business, they may not give their permission, and then the boss is safe.

Of course, it does not always work this way. Take the case of John Gotti, who basically went around to other captains in the Gambino family, persuaded them it was necessary they support his campaign to become the boss, got the bosses of a couple of other families to go along with his plan, and then dispatched four men to gun down the boss, Paul Castellano, and his underboss, Thomas Bilotti, outside Sparks Steak House in midtown Manhattan right in the heart of rush hour. It is generally regarded as one of the ballsiest and best organized hits in the history of the mob. Ballsy, because Gotti acted without the support of all the other bosses. What Gotti did do was get all his captains together and consolidate his power and basically grant himself the authority to unseat Castellano and become boss—no meeting with the Commission, no election, no nothing. Just Big Paulie lying half in the gutter on 46th Street. Gotti didn't get permission, because Gotti was a fucking wild man. Like I said, to become the boss, you really got to want it, and John Gotti really wanted it.

It goes without saying, therefore, that even the boss is not immune from getting whacked. Like kings and presidents and prime ministers and any leader, the boss is human and can be eliminated. Maybe it's a little harder to get to the boss than it is to whack an ordinary wiseguy. But it is far from impossible to penetrate a boss's ring of security and whack him. In the history of the Mafia, there have been some pretty dramatic slayings of bosses—Castellano outside Sparks; Galante gunned down in the courtyard of his favorite restaurant; Carlo Gambino arranging the execution of Albert Anastasia in a Manhattan barbershop; Lucky Luciano setting up his Genovese boss, Joe Masseria. Some would say the greatest mob hit of an elected leader was the JFK assassination, but that's another story. The point, as Michael Corleone so memorably said, is that, if history has taught us anything, it is that you can kill anybody.

I certainly experienced the madness and uncertainty of a leadership change during my time as Donnie Brasco. After the Bonanno family's longtime boss, Joe Bonanno, was forced to retire to Tucson, Arizona, under the threat of being whacked, three consecutive bosses either stepped down for health reasons or died of natural causes. Then Carmine Galante got whacked in 1979. After that, Rusty Rastelli was the boss, even though he was in jail much of the time I was undercover. According to the government, when three Bonanno wiseguys organized an attempt to remove Rastelli from power, my captain, Sonny Black, got together with Joey Massino and some other wiseguys and killed the three plotters. Rusty remained the unopposed boss of the family, but the killings led to a brief family war, as a way to settle things down.

There you have the four ways a vacancy occurs in the top job: natural death, jail, assassination, or retirement. A Mafia boss can indeed step down from the job, which is not the same as leaving the Mafia. No one can leave the Mafia under any circumstances other than death, natural or otherwise. But a boss can decide that he has had enough or is too unhealthy to continue, or simply wants to spend more time with his family, and step down as boss. Joe Bonanno's retirement was hardly voluntary, but I guess it counts as a retirement nonetheless.

So now you are a Mafia boss—now what? Believe it or not, running a hugely profitable crime family does not mean that you, yourself, are going to live like a prince. The fact is most mob bosses keep extremely low profiles and lead fairly modest lifestyles. John Gotti lived in his same little house in Ozone Park, Queens, forever. Chin

Gigante lived down in Soho like a bum. Most bosses hate publicity and attention, and having a big house somewhere just makes you a bigger target. Of course, there are exceptions—Paul Castellano lived in a big fucking mansion on Staten Island. Look where that got him.

How a boss lives depends on the boss. Like I said, low-key is the norm. All the old-time bosses—Joe Bonanno, Carlo Gambino, Vito Genovese, Vincent "Chin" Gigante—stayed way under the radar and out of the limelight. They did not spend lavishly or party late into the night. They certainly did not enjoy the spoils and perks of your typical corporate CEO. Basically, their lifestyles were not all that different from those of the wiseguys beneath them—scams, card games, good food, girlfriends, families, maybe even church on Sunday. These bosses wielded their power quietly and without fanfare—they were the opposite of media stars. I mean, can you imagine a less glamorous and dashing figure than Chin Gigante, slouching around the village in his bathrobe and slippers?

Nor does your typical boss interact all that much with other wiseguys. They do not usually hang out at the social club (again, Gotti was an exception—he spent all fucking day at his Ravenite Social Club). They do not go bouncing every night with one of their crews. They do not hit the clubs at all hours of the nights. To most wiseguys, the boss is a remote and shadowy figure—much talked about, but seldom seen. Can an ordinary soldier get in to see the boss? Not likely. I can't think of many reasons that would justify a meeting between a soldier and a boss. Can wiseguys get in to see a boss in his home? Doesn't happen. A captain gets to see the boss a couple of times a week to discuss business and hand over money, usually at a club or restaurant. But the boss is typically so far undercover that a wiseguy, even a captain, might not see him for weeks.

The inner circle around a boss is, generally, very small. He might be friends with a particular captain and keep him close at hand, and he will have his underboss and his consigliere. Maybe he has a wiseguy who is his driver. And, of course, he will have his trusted bodyguards. It really isn't like you see it in the movies, where a Mafia boss will be surrounded by goons with guns. Most bosses keep one or two bodyguards, and that's it. It's not like they're going to the supermarket to buy groceries or otherwise exposing themselves all that much. Like I said, most bosses stick close to home and try not to put themselves in the line of fire too often. Plus, they know that if their time is up—if someone really wants to get rid of them—no amount of bodyguards is going to make a difference. Remember, Galante was set up to be murdered by the very men he trusted most—his bodyguards.

The job description for a boss is not all that complicated. He will be called on to settle family disputes, promote and demote soldiers, decide on directions the family might take, make sure family profit centers are not lost or compromised. Beyond that, the boss doesn't have to do much but sit back and count the money that comes his way. Plenty of times, wiseguys get upset because they don't think the boss is doing enough to earn the money he gets. But, like most captains of industry, mob bosses are idea men, not grunts. They have already put in their years of hijacking and hustling and murdering. Now, it is time for them to rest on their reputations and dispense wisdom, not bullets.

Of course, once a wiseguy, always a wiseguy, and so, many bosses have their own illegal activities going on the side. If you've got a good thing going, you're not going to give it up just because you're the boss. Maybe the boss has a nice little bookmaking operation—no reason to cut off that revenue. Depends on how enterprising—and greedy—the boss is. In a way, you kind of hope your boss is running scams on the side, because if he doesn't have money coming in from that source, he might just ask for an increase in the weekly payments he gets from his captains, and that makes everyone's life miserable. A boss does not have to get anyone's approval to ask for more money from his captains—he is the absolute ruler and he answers to no one. Until, that is, he gets too greedy and the captains begin plotting his demise.

And since a boss can continue to run illegal operations, he can most certainly be arrested, convicted, and sent to jail. Happens all the time. Many, many mob bosses have spent five, ten, fifteen years behind bars. Such is the respect afforded a boss that being sent to jail is not considered grounds for dismissal. Like I said, some bosses feel they can't be as effective as they want to be in jail, and so they step aside and let someone else run the family, either until they get out, or permanently, depending on their sentence. But others will continue to operate as boss while in prison. Bosses can and have run crime families from behind bars. They have ways of getting shit out. The feds cannot totally shut a boss down simply by putting him in jail. He is still a citizen and he has the same right as other prisoners, and so he is entitled to have visitors. A convicted felon will not be allowed to visit, and that rules out most captains. But the boss's family—his wife and brothers, his sons and cousins—are all entitled to come and see him in jail. That is how the boss passes along his decisions and issues his orders and commands. There will also be an acting boss on the outside who most likely handles a lot of the day-to-day business. But the boss will still be the boss, and his word will still be the final word on all important matters. Perhaps a boss is a little more susceptible to being unseated while he is in prison, simply because he is out of the loop and perceived as a little less powerful. But unseating a boss who is in prison is by no means any easier than getting rid of a boss who is free. Just ask the three wiseguys whacked by Sonny Black after they conspired to unseat a jailed Rusty Rastelli.

Basically, the boss is the living embodiment of the Mafia's guiding principles—fear, intimidation, and murder. The boss can decide if he wants someone killed, and that person will be whacked, no questions asked. A boss is a dictator, not a committee leader—what he says, goes. If you are a wiseguy, you know full well that your life is in the hands of the boss of the family. Besides tyrants and despots in third world countries, what leaders have this kind of power over their subordinates? This is why wiseguys never, ever disrespect their superiors and particularly not their bosses. They will bend over backwards to be seen as loyal and respectful. You got guys who have fifteen, twenty hits under their belts—big, tough wiseguys, and they still don't move a muscle without getting the okay of their boss or underboss. You got cold-blooded killers opening car doors for their bosses, carrying their luggage, basically acting like their valets. You could have a table full of top wiseguys and not one of them is going to dare get up without first asking permission from the boss. Doesn't matter how many years you've been in the mob or how much money you've made or how many guys you've whacked—wiseguys are still required to show the proper respect to their bosses. You will never, ever catch a good wiseguy ignoring the pecking order in their family, and that means treating the boss like he's Jesus Christ himself.

Which explains me and Lefty and all those other wiseguys showing up outside that restaurant to pay our respects to—and insure the safety of—the boss of the family. So exalted is the position of the Mafia boss that most wiseguys will not even *think* bad things about them, much less say them aloud. You do not want to go around bad-mouthing the boss, because if you do, fughedaboudit. You don't know who is or isn't a fucking snitch, so you can't be sure what you say will not make it back to the boss. Insulting the boss, even in passing, can easily get you killed.

Even so, Lefty couldn't help but disparage Carmine Galante right outside the restaurant that night we stood guard. "Lilo is a mean son of a bitch, a tyrant," he told me. "Lot of people hate him. There's a lot of people out there who would like to see him get whacked." Of course, Lefty was quick to add, "That's just me telling you, it don't go no further." What he was saying may have been true, but he knew enough not to say it to anyone but a wiseguy he trusted fully. You could say Lefty was extremely lucky that I was an undercover FBI agent and not a real wiseguy with some tie to Carmine Gallante. Had I been the latter, Lefty would have been dead within days.

15

HOW WISEGUYS GET STRAIGHTENED OUT

The Mafia is not an equal-opportunity employer. To be inducted into a Mafia family, you have to be a white male of Italian descent. What that means is that your father has to be a full Italian. If your father is full Italian, you are considered an Italian. There are no exceptions to this requirement.

Before you can become a made man, before you can even be considered for indoctrination, you must go through an apprenticeship. The apprenticeship shows that you are willing to make sacrifices for the Mafia, that you are a good thief, that you have an ability to earn money. Mobsters want to see that you are a good earner, because if you're not, you can forget about ever becoming a made man. The bottom line with wiseguys is always—*always*—money.

Once your superiors see that you have a knack for making money, that you are a good and consistent earner who always shows up with a hefty envelope, then you are one step closer to being made. The next step, unfortunately, is a little trickier.

To become a made man, you have to make your bones. Which means you have to kill someone.

And we're not talking about some random killing—a noisy neighbor you iced or a bumbling burglar you blew away. We're talking about someone who is slated by the mob to be killed. What happens is that you will be told to accompany the crew member who was awarded the contract, and you will be told to assist them in carrying out the hit. The reason they do this is to make sure that you are not an undercover law enforcement officer. Wiseguys know that a law-enforcement guy is not going to go out and kill someone to become a made man. In my case, I was awarded the contract to kill a guy. But before the hit could go down, my undercover operation was terminated. Lucky me.

Once you have followed orders and participated in a hit, the path is clear for you to be proposed for membership in the family. In the old days, you had to be proposed by a made man in order to be considered for induction. But then I came along. As a direct result of my infiltration of the Bonanno crime family, and the fact that I got within a few weeks of being indoctrinated into the family, the rules for membership have been changed. Now, you must be vouched for by *two* made men, not just one. The reasoning is that it is far less likely that two guys would put their lives on the line to get you made. With just one guy, he could be sloppy or have his judgment clouded and vouch for a guy like me, Donnie Brasco. But the odds are greater that two guys would be similarly duped. That's the thinking, anyway.

Now you have proven yourself to be a good earner, and you have been proposed for membership by a made guy. Next, the commission opens up the books and tells the families they can induct new members at such and such a time; say, in a few weeks or months. Your name is entered into the books. Days, weeks, maybe even months may pass. And then one day, without warning of any kind, you will be told to be at a certain place at a certain time. You are not told why you are being summoned, but you are told to come dressed. That is how you know your day has come.

You take a shower and slick back your hair and put on your best shirt and suit. You arrive at the appointed place and you see all the capos are there. You walk into the room and the guy who proposed you takes you around and introduces you to all the capos.

You are asked if you know why you have been called. The correct answer is, "No, I do not."

You look around the room and you see a table off to the side. Placed on the table are a gun, a knife, and a picture of a saint. If you didn't know it already, now you know that you are there to be straightened out—to be inducted into the honor society. You will be walked over to the table, and then the time to recite your oath is upon you.

The made guys will ask you a series of questions. You are being asked to pledge your allegiance to the family. You must declare that you will put the Mafia before anything else in your life. Before your family, before your country, before your religion, whatever. The understanding is that once you become a made member, you will do whatever is asked of you, however difficult that assignment might be. You are expected to make whatever sacrifices are required. If it means accepting a contract to kill your own nephew or brother-in-law or even your own brother, then that's what it means. No made man is ever going to turn down a contract to kill his own brother. If he does, he knows that at some point in time, some other wiseguy is going to get the contract to whack him.

This is what is being asked of you on the day of your induction: do you understand the nature of the commitment you are making? The somber ritual of induction is intended to convey that this is deadly serious business, tested by time and passed on down through the centuries. Becoming a made man is basically like signing over your soul to the devil. There is absolutely no turning back.

And so you are told to recite an oath along these lines: "Do you swear allegiance to this family, to this thing of ours?" Yes, you answer, I do. "Does this thing of ours come before anything—God, country, family?" Yes, you say, it does. With that, the oath of *omerta* is administered, under the penalty of death. That means that if you ever betray the confidence of the family, if you ever discuss business with anyone outside the family, or rat someone out, or in any way breach the total secrecy required of wiseguys, you are in effect signing your own death certificate.

To emphasize this point, a wiseguy will prick your finger with the knife and draw a spot of blood. They will then prick the finger of the guy who proposed you and join your bloody finger with his. You are now symbolically joined to your new Mafia family.

Finally, you are handed the picture of a saint, and the picture is set on fire. While it burns in your hand, you are made to swear an oath to the family. "If I ever betray this organization," you say, "may I burn in the fires of hell."

And then it's over. You are now a made member of the family, a true wiseguy. You go around, and you kiss everybody, and everybody kisses you back. It is the most important day of your life.

16

HOW WISEGUYS
GET RESPECT

"Donnie, we need you in the back for a minute."

That is something no wiseguy, and certainly no undercover FBI agent, ever wants to hear. They were calling me into the back room of our social club for a private meeting. Wiseguys know that such a request can mean one of two things. Either there is legitimate family business that needs to be discussed in private, or you're going to get whacked.

No trip to the back room of a social club or to the basement of a mobster's house is taken without the thought that this could be the last trip you'll ever take. That's just the reality of being a wiseguy: death may be lurking behind the next closed door. Even so, there's nothing you can do but take a deep breath and go where you're told. And, most importantly, keep your cool.

So I walked into the back of Jilly's social club and encountered a roomful of wiseguys with grim mugs. As I mentioned earlier, they were there to grill me on my identity: was I really who I said I was, Donnie Brasco? I wasn't known to a lot of people, wasn't someone from the neighborhood. The time had come for my new friends to give me the third degree, guns on the table and all doors locked.

They asked me question after question designed to slip me up. Where did I grow up? Who did I know? Where did I sell my swag? Where did I do my time? I didn't act indignant or get all flustered—I answered all the questions, slowly, patiently. After a while, the temperature level in the room dropped enough for everyone to relax. The wiseguys grilling me realized they wouldn't need to put a bullet in my head. After about six hours, the meeting was over, and I walked back into the main room of the social club with three of the lower-level wiseguys who had grilled me. Now, here is where things got a little nuts.

What I did, the minute we left the back and walked into the main room, was pick out the one guy out of the three who wasn't a made man.

Then I fucking coldcocked him.

I hit this guy as hard as I could right in his face. I felt his nose collapse under my fist. He went down in a heap. Then I jumped him and rained a few more blows on his head. We rolled around on the floor for a while before the other guys broke us up. I didn't need to tell the guy why I was beating the crap out of him, but I did anyway.

"You call me a snitch, you piece of shit? You call me a fucking snitch?"

You see, the worse thing you can say about a wiseguy is that he is a snitch. Once they pulled me in the back and interrogated me on the assumption I was a snitch, they left me no choice but to react the way I did. If I hadn't been upset that I had been called a snitch—if I had reacted all thankful and giddy with my inquisitors—that might even have aroused more suspicion. By reacting the way I did, I gained a lot of credibility in the eyes of the members of the Colombo crime family. And the reason this is so can be explained in a single word:

Respect.

The foundation of the entire Mafia structure is respect. Fear is the engine, and money is the fuel. But the longevity of the Mafia as an enterprise is built upon an abiding and uncommon sense of respect. Wiseguys talk all the time about respect, about giving it and getting it in proper measures. To truly succeed as a wiseguy you must master the delicate ins and outs of the concept of respect.

As an undercover agent, I had to be extra careful to respect figures of authority while at the same time not being too deferential to anyone. There is giving people the proper amount of respect, and then there is being a pussy. A wiseguy is very respectful to authority, but no wiseguy worth his salt lays down for anyone. That is why I had to pop one of the guys who called me a snitch. He had profoundly disrespected me by grilling me the way he did and insinuating I might be a rat. It was essential that I make some sort of statement that showed I not only knew I had been disrespected but that I was not going to put up with that kind of treatment. In the end, the best way to gain and keep respect is to stand up for yourself. I will give you a couple more examples of what I mean by that.

After breaking my Donnie Brasco cover, I did a lot of undercover work for Scotland Yard in London. The cops over there were after the Triads, a mean bunch of fuckers and the most notorious gang in England. These Triads were making millions counterfeiting credit cards in a factory in Hong Kong and shipping phony Amex, Visa, and Mastercards all across the world. A couple of Scotland Yard detectives had gone undercover to deal with the gang, but they were still having a hard time getting their hooks into the top guys. Most of all, they wanted to get to the top guy at the factory in Hong Kong, a guy who was the Number 2 man in the entire Triad organization. Try as they might, they just couldn't get close to this boss. I had worked for Scotland Yard before. I knew their guys, and I had taught at their school, so they called me up and asked if I could lend a hand. The undercover British cops wanted me to pretend to be the New York wiseguy who was the boss they answered to. That way, they could go to this No. 2 man and tell them their boss was in town. I agreed, and the undercover cops set up a meeting between me and No. 2.

The meeting was set for a big suite in a big resort. The suite was fully bugged and monitored, and a surveillance team was in the room next door. Before I go in the British detective sergeant in charge of the operation pulls me aside and starts to tell me how I should handle the Triad. The sergeant is a nice guy, a little on the nervous side, and I'm sure he's never worked a day undercover in his life. Still, he's telling me how to act around the Triad, how to talk, how to look, on and on. I tell him, "Look, I'm the undercover guy, I'll do the undercover work. You do the administrative work. I don't have to be told how to talk to a gangster. I know how much respect to show him and how much respect he has to show me." That pretty much settles that matter.

The start of the meeting comes and goes without me there. I arrive late, on purpose, to show this Triad that although we are technically equal, I am just a little better than him. I walk into the hotel suite and the two British undercovers are there, along with No. 2. After the introductions we all sit down and go through the motions of getting to know each other. After a while, we talk business. The Triad tells me how each phony credit card can be used for about ten thousand dollars before it's banged out. I tell him that I want to increase our purchase of these cards. I also explain how, before I increase my order, I will need to see the operation up close. I will not put up all this money without having complete confidence that the Triads can supply me with all the cards I need in New York. I will have to see the Hong Kong factory firsthand. We go back and forth on this point, and it's not clear if No. 2 is going to agree to my terms.

That's when I notice that this guy is interrupting me.

I mean, every time I say something, this guy interrupts with his own thought. We're going on and on with discussions and I can't finish a fucking sentence. Finally, in the middle of something he's saying, I pull him up short.

"Hey, let me ask you a question," I say. "Why do all of your sentences start in the middle of mine?"

The two British undercovers drop their jaws to the floor. No. 2 looks at me like he doesn't know what to say. I go on.

"Don't you have any respect?" I say. "Don't you know who you're talking to?" The guy still doesn't have an answer for me. "In my world," I continue, "we have respect for one another and we let each other finish our sentences. If you're going to continue starting your sentences in the middle of mine, I'm leaving. And until you decide you're going to show me the respect you should be showing somebody of my status, I'm not coming back."

I get up to leave. The British cops don't know what to do. The big shot from the Triads finally opens his mouth. What comes out is a total apology.

"I'm sorry, I'm sorry, I meant no disrespect," he says. "Please forgive me. I'm sorry, I'm sorry." He starts calling me "mister." The guy is just about groveling at this point. I sit back down.

As it turns out, we get that invitation to tour the Hong Kong factory. The guy gives us the location of the factory and everything, and Scotland Yard eventually shuts it down. The boys in the next suite later tell me they practically had heart attacks when I pulled this No. 2 guy up short. Certainly the guy could have just got up and left, killing the deal forever. But just the opposite happened. Once he discovered that I was his equal, that I was maybe even a notch or two above him, we were able to converse on an even footing. Once he learned how to *respect* me, he agreed to invite me into his factory. But it took my threatening demand for respect to make it happen. I understood that this is how wiseguys get respect, that to wiseguys respect is everything. Without it, you are not only at a disadvantage, but you just might get yourself killed.

Another time, I was working undercover in Las Vegas. Again, I was supposed to be this big wiseguy from New York. We rented a huge suite at one of the casino hotels and set up a meeting between me and two real wiseguys. I show up, and we're all sitting around talking about this and that, and everything is going pretty smoothly.

Until one of the wiseguys puts his feet up on the coffee table.

I look at him and I say, "What are you doing?"

He looks at me and says, "What?"

I say, "What are you doing with your feet up on the coffee table?"

The guy says, "I'm just trying to get comfortable."

"Do you put your feet up on the furniture at home?"

"Well, no."

"Then why the fuck are you putting them up on the furniture here? This is my suite, this is where I live. What the fuck are you doing putting your feet up on the furniture and disrespecting me like that?"

The other undercover guys look mortified. The real wiseguy looks about the same. "Whoa, whoa, I didn't mean it, I was just trying to get comfortable," he stammers. "No disrespect, no disrespect, please, accept my apology."

I say, "Next time, show a little respect and act like a gentleman. Cause if my boss come in and sees you with your feet up on the furniture, he's going to think, 'What the fuck kind of lowlife is this guy?'"

That was all it took. I now had his complete respect. I demanded it, and I received it. Everything was easier after that. Of course, my little power play was not without risk. Had this guy had half a ball, he could have popped me for being disrespectful to him. But that was a chance I was willing to take. In life, you will be accorded precisely the respect that you demand for yourself. Once you learn that lesson, you are way ahead of the game.

17

HOW WISEGUYS TAKE OVER A BUSINESS

Hostile takeover has a whole different meaning when it comes to wiseguys. This is how they go about merging someone else's business with their own.

You pick a place. Bars are great targets for wiseguys because they're a cash business with plenty of opportunity for hiding profits. So, you pick a bar that's doing pretty good and you send two wiseguys in. The wiseguys hang around, strike up a conversation with the barkeep, get to know the manager, come across as regular guys. You do this for two, three days in a row. The fourth day, you step things up.

The fourth day, one of the wiseguys goes up to the manager and broaches the subject of insurance protection. You explain how it would be smart to pay for insurance against rowdy patrons who could damage your establishment and drive away business and maybe even wreck the place. You do this knowing that nobody is going to buy this line, that anybody with half a brain is going to see this pitch as extortion, plain and simple. You know the manager is going to tell you to get lost. You finish your drinks and you go.

You come back the fifth night with two more wiseguys, which makes four of you in all. The original two wiseguys sit at the bar and order their drinks. The two new wiseguys come in and sit next to them at the bar and start an argument. The argument gets louder and louder, and before you know it, the two new wiseguys are going at each other pretty good. The wiseguys start to kick each other's ass, and they basically wreck the place. Crash into tables, throw chairs, break bottles, knock over stunned patrons. Nothing anybody can do to stop it. The two original wiseguys sit at the bar and enjoy the show for a while, then jump in and break up the "fight." They save the day and send the other wiseguys on their way. Then they find the manager and pull him over for another chat.

Once again, they broach the subject of insurance protection.

Of course, the manager knows what's going on, knows the fight was staged. If he doesn't, if he's a little slow on the uptake, maybe he tells the wiseguys to get lost again. Then the other wiseguys come back in a couple of nights later and wreck the place all over again. But more than likely the manager knows enough to accept the wiseguys' deal. There are no negotiations. By the sixth day, the wiseguys are getting whatever fee they asked for—collectible weekly—to protect the place.

In less than a week, a fresh new stream of income has been generated with no more investment than the price of a few drinks.

This is the most popular way to take over a business, but it is not the only way. Wiseguys are opportunistic; if they see another way in, they will jump all over it. Perhaps they learn that the owner of a particular business has some kind of weakness. Say he's a degenerate gambler. You make sure one of your bookies begins handling his bets. You give him favorable treatment, and you let him gamble himself into a big hole, and you allow him to run up a big fat debt, and then you go in and ask him to settle up. Naturally, the guy can't pay. You discuss assuming part of his business as a settlement. Once you have your hooks in the business, you suck all the money you can out of it until you milk it dry. You leave the ravaged carcass of a once thriving enterprise in your wake.

Say the guy has a coke problem. Even easier. You supply the guy with the best drugs around and let him run up a big fucking tab. A coke addict cannot see past the white dust on the end of his nose. You approach the guy for the money he owes you, and you make him choose between surrendering part of his business or surrendering part of his spleen. Then, once again, you treat the business like your own personal ATM.

Another way in: the owner of a business needs a quick loan. The bank turns him down; his friends turn him down; he has nowhere else to turn. You send a shylock over and press a big wad of cash in his hand. The vig, or interest, is exorbitant, but most entrepreneurs have an inordinate faith in their own business savvy and as a result make easy marks. You, on the other hand, know full well the guy will not be able to make his payments. The vig compounds daily, the guy misses a payment or two and very quickly he is in a bottomless hole. You move in and take a percentage of his business. No contract, no lawyers, no deal points. Just pain and shame if you're the owner and easy money for the mobsters.

Some guys go to Harvard Business School for three years to learn how to turn a profit. Wiseguys produce unbelievable cash flow in a week.

18

HOW WISEGUYS
CARRY OUT A HIT

Murder is the cornerstone on which the vast Mafia empire is built. Whacking someone is the most vivid and dramatic illustration of the wiseguy way of doing business. Arranging to have someone killed is the most coldly efficient method of dealing with sticky problems, and—since wiseguys are the only entrepreneurs willing to go to such extremes to keep things running smoothly—it's the principal thing that separates mobsters from other crooked businessmen. The cold-blooded hit would be the sordid underbelly of the wiseguy way of life, if only that way of life wasn't one big underbelly to begin with.

This, then, is how a hit goes down.

First, the order for a hit comes down, usually from the boss of the family. The order can come from a captain, but the captain has to get an okay from the boss first. The only time a wiseguy will ever kill someone is on orders from the boss or the captain. Killing people without direct orders is something that you do at your own risk.

As for the target, you can be sure that the person getting hit is either a wiseguy or someone doing business with a wiseguy. Wiseguys are not in the business of whacking random people, or whacking people out of petty grudges. John Gotti allegedly getting rid of the poor bastard who accidentally ran over his young son was an exception. Almost without fail, the targeted person either fucked a wiseguy out of money or embarrassed a wiseguy in some way. Maybe he disrespected a made guy; maybe he got greedy in some deal. But, at least with the American Mafia, when you read about somebody getting whacked, you know that person was involved in illegal activity and made a fateful mistake along the way.

And so the order comes down. The captain passes the order along, and the assignment is doled out to one or two of the guys in his crew. A mobster does not get paid for hitting someone, so there is no negotiating a price. Murder is the dues a mobster pays to be in the club. It is simply part of your job as a wiseguy or an associate. One day, your captain will call you over and you will get the contract to kill someone. More than likely, that person is someone you know pretty well.

The reason for this is that you can get close enough to this person to whack him with relative ease. If you ever suspect that you have been targeted for a hit, keep the closest eye on your very best friends. It will always be your partner or some other guy you like and trust who will sneak up behind you and send you to your reward. In the case of Carmine Galante, the boss of the Bonanno family, they killed him in the backyard of Joe and Mary's, a restaurant in Brooklyn. You've seen the photos—Carmine sprawled on the ground, lit cigar still chomped in his mouth. His two bodyguards did not prevent the hit, mainly because they were the two guys who set it up. Surely Galante thought he was as safe as he could be, having lunch in a place owned by a close relative, with two burly bodyguards nearby. Even the boss of the family did not foresee his own betrayal. Trusting anyone is a fatal mistake for a wiseguy.

Once the order comes down, a wiseguy cannot decline the contract. It does not matter who the contract is on or what your relationship to that person is: there is no valid reason for turning a contract down. A wiseguy has pledged allegiance to the mob and vowed to kill anybody that crosses the family. One wiseguy I knew got the contract to kill his own son-in-law. This jerk was skimming drug money, and the bosses got fed up and sent word down to whack him. The contract went to the guy's father-in-law, because he could get closer than anyone to the target without arousing suspicion. Now, here's a wiseguy who not only must kill his own son-in-law but must also widow his own daughter and wipe out his own grandson's father. He knows he will be devastating those closest to him. But that is the oath you take when you join the Mafia. Mob business always comes first, ahead of family. This wiseguy shot two bullets into his own son-in-law's head. Perhaps he reasoned to himself that his daughter was better off without this piece of shit. For sure, he did not dwell on what it would be like for his grandson to wake up without a daddy.

If you get the contract to hit someone and you know that person pretty well, all the better. That means you know his routines, his hangouts, his weaknesses. If, however, you get the contract on someone you don't know too well, then the first thing you do is find out all you can about the guy. First, you grill the guy who gives you the contract. What does this guy look like; where does he live; what kind of car does he drive; what bars and restaurants does he like; who are his friends? You do *not* ask why he is being marked for death. That is not your business. Your boss will fill you in on who this poor fellow is and where he lives, and then the rest is up to you.

For the next few days, you stalk your prey. You follow him in your car; you park nearby as he walks into a restaurant; you go inside and sit at the bar and watch how this guy operates. Is he a suspicious type, always checking over his shoulder? Or is he sloppy and stupid, drinking too much and turning his back on the front door? You begin to make plans for how and where you will whack him. Eventually, you decide on a time and place. You do not go back to your captain or boss and get their approval for your plan. They do not want to know the specifics of the hit. It is entirely your decision to make, your job to succeed at or fuck up. Once you have selected a time and place, you must decide how you will end this poor fuck's life.

For New York wiseguys, the preferred method of execution is two behind the ear. Usually .22 caliber bullets. If it is a friend or associate that you are whacking, the hit is usually carried out in a car or in the back room of a private restaurant or in somebody's basement, when you are just hanging out. If the hit is in a car, you make sure your target sits in the passenger seat, so that the killer can slip into the back seat right behind him. If the hit is set up at a club or base-ment, you have to get your target there. Maybe a meeting is called to get you to the place where your executioner awaits. Being sum-moned to such a meeting is always a dreadful occasion for gangsters. In the backs of their minds they know that they could be stepping into a trap which will cost them, well, the backs of their minds. But they have no choice but to show up.

One time, I was called to a meeting in the back room of a restaurant. The door was closed and locked behind me, and at that very instant I knew that there was a very good chance the only way I would leave that room was wrapped in a rug. Sure enough, the wiseguys who brought me to the room wanted to know if I was real-ly who I said I was: Donnie Brasco, jewel thief. They grilled me about where I came from, who I knew, what sort of jobs I pulled, all of that. I really had to prove that I was Donnie Brasco, and if I didn't do a convincing job of it, I was good as dead. I kept my cool and pulled it off, and then the door was unlocked and we went into the main room of the restaurant. Wiseguys learn to live with the constant threat of death. If they didn't, they'd be nervous fucks who couldn't even leave their apartments.

So that is how it will go: you will be summoned to a meeting. Wiseguys are not interested in gunfights or hand-to-hand combat. They want a clean hit, no struggle, no fuss. Once you are in the room, they will slink up silently behind you and level their pistols to the back of your head and coldly pull the trigger. No grand speeches, no: "This is for fucking us over, scumbag." Just the blast of a gunshot and the splatter of brains and blood. The bullet will bore through your skull and ravage your brain matter and maybe exit through your eye and drop you dead to the ground. Once you are down, they will likely fire a second slug into your brain. Maybe afterwards someone will call you a scumbag and say, "It's done." Wiseguys will kill you that way.

Of course, there are other ways besides gunshots to cook a chicken. Take the case of Chicken Man Testa, the boss of the Angelo Bruno family in Philadelphia. Wiseguys in Philadelphia are a little more violent and will use bombs for a lot of hits. Gangsters in the Midwest—Detroit, Chicago—have no compunction about planting bombs under your cars; in fact, it's their favorite thing. Chicken Man Testa triggered a nail bomb as he walked up the steps of his front porch and was blown into a million pieces. Mobsters in New York City are a little more sophisticated and pretty much stick to pistols. Except, that is, for the New York wiseguy who came up with the idea of whacking someone by riding past him on a motorcycle and stabbing him with an infected hypodermic needle. That wiseguy never got the chance to try out his brilliant idea.

Using a bomb, of course, takes care of the body. No need to go back and scrape up the scattered limbs. When you shoot a guy, however, you then have to dispose of the body. Generally, you wrap the guy up in a rug and load him into your trunk. Maybe he only fits in the front seat, so you put him there. Where you dump him depends on what message is being sent. If it's just a straight hit with no particular message attached, you will dump the body somewhere it is not likely to be found. If wiseguys don't want you to be found, they will cut you up with a chainsaw and stick your body parts in green plastic trash bags and drive you to the ocean and dump you in the water. Maybe they put you into steel compactors and turn you into a car fender. Sometimes, whacked mobsters turn up in weird spots. Some ingenious New Jersey wiseguys carved false bottoms into real coffins and stashed an extra body inside. The pallbearers might have been surprised at how heavy the coffin was, but in the end, the legitimate stiff and the mystery stiff both got buried. Most of the time, murdered wiseguys simply go missing, and their bodies—or body parts—are never found.

Dismembering a guy is also a way of sending a message. If that's the case, then your body will not be discarded but left somewhere it can be found. If, say, you were a snitch, they might cut off your prick and stick it in your mouth. My own captain, Sonny Black, the guy who introduced me to other crime bosses, was whacked shortly after my identity was made public. His body was found with his two hands cut off. He had taken me around and allowed me to shake hands with top mob figures. For that, he not only lost his life but also lost his hands.

When wiseguys do not bother to dispose of a body, that is a way to send a message. Tony Mirra, the other made man who was killed because of my infiltration of the mob, was shot in his car and left in his car in a parking garage in an apartment building, like he was nobody. The way police could be sure it was a mob hit was because he still had all his money and jewelry. Wiseguys will never take anything after a hit—not your money, not your watch, nothing. Leaving Tony Mirra in his car, in a puddle of his own blood, was a way to let other gangsters know that making the same mistakes Tony made would, to say the least, not be looked on favorably.

Once you have disposed of the body—or not—the hit is complete. And once the hit is complete, you never, ever talk about it. There is no bragging, no discussion. Once the guy is dead, you never hear about him again. He's dead, he's gone, that's it. It's like he never existed. Nor is there any remorse over killing the guy. Right after a hit, a wiseguy will ask his partner, "Where are we going for dinner?" I have known of several guys who, immediately after whacking someone, went out and had a big Italian pasta dinner. To wiseguys, murder is just another bit of business to handle. Why let it spoil your appetite?

19

A TYPICAL DAY
IN THE
LIFE OF A WISEGUY

Say no jobs are planned for the day, which is the case most days. No runs, no special meeting, no hits. This is how the day unfolds.

A wiseguy gets up in the morning at nine-thirty, maybe ten. Guys who are pigeon fanciers, they go up to the roof to feed the birds. Guys who fool around with tropical fish, they feed the fish and maintain the tank. Lots of wiseguys are into either pigeons or fish. You finish with that, you have some coffee, maybe a hard roll with butter. Plenty of butter. You shower, and you are out of the house by eleven-thirty, maybe noon.

You go to the club—the social club. Everybody meets at the social club. From the outside it looks like nothing—an unmarked door, no window. From the inside, it doesn't look much better: a brass coffeemaker in the corner, some booze behind the bar, a few cheap chairs and tables, and a room in the back for serious business. And that's about it. You hang around the club playing cards and shooting the shit. You play gin rummy; wiseguys love gin rummy. You talk about scores that you're going to pull, scores that you should have pulled, scores that you're thinking of pulling. You talk about deals that went down, deals that went wrong, rackets you should be running better. If you run numbers, you talk about the numbers for the day. If you're a loan shark, you talk about the loans. Bookies talk about point spreads. Everybody talks about who has the power and how they can usurp that power. You talk about feuds within the family, feuds with other families, feuds with other wiseguys. Wiseguys do not talk about what most people talk about: how's the family? Where are you vacationing this year? Do you know a good dentist? Wiseguys talk about what's going on in the Mafia, what illegal business transactions are coming up, and how they are going to steal their next buck. The conversation is almost entirely about mob business. Guys playing cards, guys coming and going, guys talking to other guys about deals and rackets, guys from other families talking about *their* deals and rackets, guys playing cards and talking about their deals and rackets at the same time.

Then it's lunchtime.

Around two or two-thirty, wiseguys order lunch. Wiseguys like Chinese food. Maybe you send out for Chinese. Or maybe a big Italian hero. You eat lunch, and you walk around the neighborhood a little, and then you go back to the club and play cards again.

Then it's dinnertime.

Around five or six, everybody goes home. You do what you have to do with your family. You have dinner, talk to your wife a little, put your kids to bed. Then, around nine or nine-thirty, you go back to the social club. Lots of jobs go down at night, so if you have a job to pull, you do it. Otherwise, you meet the guys and you all go to a nightclub, and you spend a couple of hours bouncing around from club to club. Maybe you go to a restaurant and have a second dinner. You do this with other wiseguys, or you do it with other wiseguys and all your girlfriends, your *gumatas*.

Finally, around two or two-thirty in the morning, you call it quits. Everybody goes home and goes to sleep. Next morning, you get up and you do it all over again. Same exact way.

The life of a wiseguy is very repetitious. Every day is just like the next day, except Sunday. Sunday is the day you spend with your family. Friday night, you take out your *gumata*. Saturday nights, you go out for a night on the town with your wife. Sundays, you spend the whole day with your wife and kids, except for maybe a couple of hours you spend at the club. Sunday is the day that wiseguys are most like you and me. Mondays, they go back to being wiseguys.

And that's it. That's a typical day in the life of a wiseguy. Not exactly glamorous like in the movies. But you sure get good at gin rummy.

20

WISEGUY NICKNAMES

Say what you will about wiseguys, they got the best nicknames in the business. You look at the sports world and maybe one of every ten athletes has a decent nickname. Broadway Joe. Earl the Pearl. Air Jordan ain't bad. But every mobster worth a damn is going to have a good nickname. What's more, mob nicknames are very useful. They sum up a wiseguy for you better than any long-winded description ever could. You got the Dapper Don—what else you need to know about John Gotti besides he liked seeing himself on TV in expensive suits?

Then there were the guys I hung with—Sonny Black, so named because he dyed his hair jet black, and Lefty Two Guns, who . . . well, figure it out. There was Bobby Badheart, a wiseguy with a pacemaker. Frankie the Nose, a fella with a huge honker. Jimmy Legs, who had long ones. Mike the Hat, Charlie Chains, Nick the Stick, Sonny Smash. Willie Smokes, Tommy Scar, Joey Burns, Tommy Twitch. Tony the Sheik, Frank the Bug, Ronnie the Pig, Willie the Rat. Joey Half Ball, Nicky Cigars, Tony Ducks, Mickey Spats. Dago Mike and Dago Louie. Fat Tony and Skinny Pete. Lead-Pipe Joe and Tony the Hatchet. Little Bozo, Joey Gags, Joey the Clown, and Charlie Bananas. You got The Beak, The Snake, The Owl, and The Butcher. Louie HaHa, Phil Lucky, Vinny Oil, Tony Roach. Some particularly colorful guys had as many as three nicknames. Bonanno underboss Nicky Marangello was Nicky Cigars, Nicky Glasses, and Little Nicky—take your pick. Lots of times, guys don't even know your last name. All they know you by is your nickname.

Me? Sometimes they called me Donnie the Jeweler. Because, big surprise, my cover was that I was a jewel thief. An okay nickname, but not great. Beats Donnie Dimples on His Ass, I guess.

21

WHAT WISEGUYS SAY AND WHAT THEY MEAN

"I **got to get back in shape. Got to go lift weights."** When a normal person says this, it means he's going to the gym. When a wiseguy says it, it means he's going to jail.

Wiseguys think of jail as a chance to get three square meals a day and finally improve on their pitiful physical condition. To them, a prison stretch is a vacation from their nagging wives, their equally nagging girlfriends, their noisy families, their endless work hassles. Not a bad deal, overall. That's why, if a wiseguy tells you, "I've got to get away, go to a resort," it doesn't mean he's booked a week at Club Med. It means he's doing five to ten at Sing Sing.

Every group of like-minded people has its own terminology and slang. But wiseguys take it to a whole other level. Maybe half of everything a wiseguy says will be in wiseguy lingo. For me to make a decent undercover mafioso, I had to soak up a fucking dictionary full of wiseguy sayings. Some of them are just funny little ways of putting things. Some derive from the fact that wiseguys can be pretty stupid.

For instance, a wiseguy might tell you, "That babbo has a parakeet down in Pepsi Cola." Huh? Means some useless underling has a mistress down in Pensacola. Or he might say, "I killed two stones, so now it's water under the drain." Means he killed two birds with one stone, and now it's water under the bridge. And God forbid you ask a wiseguy what he means when he tells you, "I had to give a ham and cheese samich to the deli." If he discovers you don't know that means he had to give payoff to a union delegate, he's liable to "make a fucking indication of youse on the wall" (figure it out).

Wiseguys have their own, quirky language. Start with the Italian. *La cosa nostra*, of course, is Italian for "this thing of ours," which is how wiseguys refer to the Mafia. *Consigliere* is Italian for "counselor," the title awarded to a Mafia boss's closest adviser. *Omerta*: the Italian word that represents the Mafia's code of silence.

These are Mobspeak 101, familiar to anyone who's seen *The Godfather*.

Then there is the corporate terminology. When wiseguys talk about the administration, they are referring to the upper-level power structure of an organized crime family: the boss, the underboss, and the consigliere. A boss is the highest designation there is in the Mafia, and no one is more powerful—except, that is, for the boss of bosses, the old-world term used to describe the strongest of the five New York crime family bosses. These five family bosses, collectively, are referred to as the "Commission," the Mafia's ruling body.

Beneath these top-level mobsters there are capos: ranking wiseguys who are in charge of a crew of soldiers. An associate is a wannabe wiseguy who is almost there but who has yet to be sworn in. And a young tough guy looking to become a made member of the mob is called a *cugine*. Now you know the basic terms that FBI agents use to identify their prey. Again, familiar to the casual *Sopranos* fan.

But there's a lot more you need to know if you plan on conversing with a wiseguy anytime soon. Any mobster worth his hair gel will never refer to his weapon as a gun or a pistol—it is always, "my piece." Wiseguys do not refer to their tax-free gambling profits— they talk about the "skim." The exorbitant interest accrued on mob loans? That would be the "vigorish," or "vig." Stolen merchandise, wiseguys will tell you, is "swag." And stockbrokers may speak of the bottom line or the gross profit, but wiseguys call it the "nut."

How about when a wiseguy says somebody is "broken"? Means the poor bastard has been demoted in rank. Being broken, however, still beats being "chased." To be chased means to be banished from the Mafia and barred from ever associating with any made member, a relatively benign sentence handed down in lieu of death. That's why being chased is preferable to being "burned," which means, simply, being whacked.

Wiseguys just love to talk around stuff. When a wiseguy says he has to "come in," that means he has been ordered to see the boss. When a wiseguy says he wants to "take a walk," it means he wants to discuss sensitive business matters while strolling in the street, so as to avoid the FBI bugs that are surely planted in the social club. Sometimes when a wiseguy isn't taking a walk he's having a "sit-down": that means he's attending a meeting of family members to resolve a dispute. The dispute may center on a "bean"—a hundred dollars—but more likely will involve a whole bunch of "crackers" (a thousand dollars).

When a wiseguy refers to an "empty suit," he's talking about a dope who hangs out with family members but brings nothing to the table himself. When a wiseguy talks about "giving a gift," it has nothing to do with somebody's anniversary—he's talking about bribing a juror. A wiseguy wants to avoid a "hot place," not because he dislikes the sun and palm trees, but because that place is under FBI surveillance. Wiseguys tend to make friends with "meat eaters," not because of their shared taste in food but because meat eaters are corrupt cops. A wiseguy can give someone a "free pass," which will not entitle the receiver to see a movie or a concert but will entitle him to draw breath, since he's been handed a reprieve from being whacked. Then again, a wiseguy may tell you he just "ate blood." Translation: he killed someone and watched them die.

This, of course, is just the beginning. Listen to a couple of hours of FBI surveillance tape, and you'll hear dozens of words you never heard before. Wiseguys do not say "et cetera"; they say "but-a-beepa-da-bopa-da-boop." As in, "This guy is a pain in the balls, he calls me every night, he bugs me at the club, but-a-beepa-da-bopa-da-boop." And why say "this and that" when you can say, "dis, dis, dis, dis, dis, and dat." You are likely to hear a wiseguy mispronounce his own hangout—the venerable social club—as a "sociable club." Similarly, wiseguys have been known to butcher pizza (beatza), groin (groan), Muenster cheese (monster cheese), cottage cheese (college cheese), fiscal year (physical year), pneumonia (ammonia), sporadic (spasmodic), and even paramour (power mower). Wiseguys don't end up in the emergency room; they go to the mercy room. And just because a wiseguy says "jew box" does not mean he's anti-Semitic: he's just talking about a juke box. Then again, most wiseguys are, indeed, anti-Semitic.

Here's a little known fact: wiseguys do not say, "Fuck you." They say, "Fuck Youse!," always at three hundred decibels. A wiseguy may say, "Good-bye, and good luck to you," but that hardly means he is being gracious. It's just his way of saying, "Get the fuck out of here." If you hear, "God bless America!," you're probably an FBI agent being told by a wiseguy to "Do what you have to do and arrest me, but leave me alone and don't ask me stupid questions." Things in wiseguy world are never impossible; they are "un-fucking-possible."

Okay, now let's talk money. As in "blood money"—any loan from a loan shark that will cause blood to be extracted if not paid back. Usually the blood will be extracted after a single missed payment of non-principal-reducing interest. Then there is "fast money"—a short-term loan-shark loan, usually a "five for nine" deal, which means a guy borrows five hundred dollars on Monday and must repay nine hundred dollars by Friday. If you've taken a "Chinese loan," you've got to pay down the exorbitant, illegal interest on the principal within thirty days. And if you've got a "knock-down loan," then too bad for you—that means if you miss a single interest payment, the loan converts to a "vig" loan, and the missed interest payment is added to the principal. That, if you haven't already figured out, can get very expensive.

But don't worry if you can't make that first interest payment. You can always borrow it down—take out an additional loan to pay off a pre-existing knockdown loan, almost always from a different loan shark.

Finally, there is that great catchall wiseguy phrase: "Forget about it." Or, as it is more accurately spelled, "fughedaboudit." This was the phrase that really baffled my fellow FBI agents when it turned up repeatedly on wiretaps during my tenure as Donnie Brasco. It was used to convey so many different sentiments, my guys just couldn't get a handle on what it really meant.

Basically, it can be used to mean anything. Perhaps the most common usage is to convey satisfaction with something, as in, "This prosciutto, fughedaboudit." To say that is to say the prosciutto was excellent. At the same time, if you think the prosciutto tastes like shoe leather, you might say, "This prosciutto, fughedaboudit." Now you understand the potential for confusion.

Similarly, if you agree with someone, you can say, "Fughedaboudit." "Some body on that broad, huh?" they say. "Fughedaboudit," you reply. But if you disagree with them, you can also say "Fughedaboudit." If you think the lady in question has a body that is less than perfect, you can reply, "That broad? Built like a cement mixer. Fughedaboudit."

And that's not all. If someone insults you, an appropriate response would be "Fughedaboudit." It's the same as telling someone to go to hell. A wiseguy cracks smart with something like, "Look at that wrinkled suit, marone, did you sleep in the Lincoln Tunnel?," you throw him a dirty look and say, simply, "Fughedaboudit."

Finally, as Johnny Depp explained in one of the most memorable scenes in *Donnie Brasco*, sometimes "fughedaboudit" means just that: forget about it.

"Should we go to his house and break his kneecaps?"

"No, fughedaboudit."

How, then, are you supposed to know what a wiseguy is talking about, what with all this mobster lingo? The answer is: you don't have to understand them. Just nod your head and say, "Fughedaboudit."

22

WISEGUYS
WORK SCAMS 24/7

Hijacking. **Loan-sharking. Bookmaking.** Slot machines. Porn parlors. Extortion. Drugs. Stock schemes. Chop shops. Money laundering. Construction fraud. Garbage collection. Garment manufacture. The bulk theft of merchandise from loading docks. These are the core enterprises of the modern Mafia.

But these are only some of the ways that wiseguys make money. Wiseguys see an opportunity for graft, corruption, and profit in almost any endeavor imaginable. When you see a wiseguy reading the newspaper, it means he's hard at work. He is searching for his next scam.

Wiseguys scheme and plot the way other people breathe and blink. They are playing the angles every second they are awake. Their health and well-being depends on them being thought of as good earners, and so any opportunity to rake in a few more dollars must be considered and pursued. No racket is beneath a wiseguy, no matter how sleazy or low-rent. Money is money is money.

For instance, I knew a wiseguy who was an absolute master of the phony injury claims, a mobster mainstay. He would wait for a city bus to roll around and walk right in front of it at the last minute. Of course, he knew what he was doing, so that while it appeared he was being hit and thrown in the air, he was really absorbing very little contact. Nevertheless, he'd wind up on the street holding his legs or side or head and screaming to concerned pedestrians, "Don't fucking touch me; I need a fucking doctor." Inevitably, insurance companies would quickly settle the claim out of court. This wiseguy was pretty good at getting run over by taxicabs, too.

If a wiseguy can rip the head off a parking meter and smash it open to steal a few quarters, he will do it. Then there is this chest-nut: the penny stock pump-and-dump. Wiseguys line up a phone bank, call unsuspecting marks touting some or other stock, drive up the price, cash in, and disappear long before anyone figures out the stock is worthless. Easy money. All you need are some phones and a few wiseguys to bully people over the phone into parting with their hard-earned dollars.

But even that is fairly labor-intensive compared to some wiseguy scams. Most famously, there was the Windows Scandal in New York City in the 1980s, a variation of the old bait-and-switch. Basically, wiseguys rigged union contracts to provide the city's crumbling schools with brand new windows. They contracted to provide one particular brand of window, then installed a vastly inferior brand. They pocketed the difference in price. Minimal investment of time, resources, and manpower—maximum profit.

Another good one: roping a hapless doctor into writing phony drug prescriptions and providing phony medical reports for fraudulent insurance claims. All wiseguys have to do is pay a couple of visits to the doctor to make sure everything is running smoothly and file the phony claims. Again, minimal investment, maximum return.

Wiseguys never stop working the angles. When they go to prison, they work the guards so they can smuggle stuff in. When they go into witness protection, they find a way to deal drugs on the side. When they go to bed, they don't count sheep, they add up the vig on shylock loans. And even when wiseguys pretend to take real jobs as a cover for their wiseguy work, they figure out how to scam money out of the real jobs, too. A couple of wiseguys I knew had no-show sanitation jobs before claiming to have fallen off their sanitation trucks and gotten injured. Believe it or not, they both collected disability and social security payments for years before somebody caught on.

If there's a way to make money, wiseguys will see it. If there's an angle to be played, wiseguys will play it. If there's a good and honest enterprise run by decent people, wiseguys will turn into a mob racket. This is what wiseguys do—they seize any opportunity to make an extra buck. There is only one rule governing their behavior—don't get caught.

Wiseguys even scam each other if they can. Lefty Ruggiero was always asking me for money, always grabbing a quick hundred here and there. Wiseguys, you see, are takers. They take whatever they can to enrich themselves, regardless of the consequences. You will never find a more opportunistic breed than wiseguys. They suck up money like vampires suck blood.

Again, there is nothing admirable about this sort of conduct. It pretty much violates any standard of decency and goodness that our society relies on to function smoothly. But once you accept the fact that wiseguys are leeches, you can take a detached look at their incredible focus on the bottom line. Sure, there are business moguls who never, ever stop dreaming up deals and making money—Donald Trump comes to mind. But most entrepreneurs are far less focused. Wiseguys have their minds on their business dealings twenty-four hours a day, seven days a week. Honest to God, even when they're sleeping, I bet they are dreaming of some scam or racket. That is certainly one of the reasons they are so successful. They are uncommonly devoted to the task of making money.

23

A FEW THINGS
WISEGUYS DON'T DO

Wiseguys don't do favors. Or, more precisely, they don't do favors the way you and I do favors. One thing you never, ever want to do as a citizen or as somebody on the fringes of the mob is to let a mobster do you a favor. Enormous mistake. A wiseguy will be more than happy to do you a favor, to bail you out of a really tight spot, to come up with money when the banks say no, to basically be a lifesaver when no one else seems to care. What's more, they will not ask anything in return for doing that favor—at least, not right away. But somewhere down the line—could be a year, could be two years, could be a couple of months—the wiseguy will call that favor in. And you better believe that the favor you are asked to do will be a lot more complicated, and involve a lot more sacrifice, than the good deed they did in the first place. They may ask you to repay the loan you took within a certain time period; say, that very day. They may ask you for a piece of your business. If you're a politician, you can be sure they will want you to pull some strings for them. And if, for some reason, you cannot oblige them, then you will incur the sort of wrath and fury that you could not have imagined in your darkest nightmares. Basically, once you have allowed a gangster to do you a favor, you have signed over your soul to them. No favor is ever, ever done without the expectation of something in return. To wiseguys, a favor is a business contract that binds you to them in perpetuity. It is a gigantic fucking trap from which you can never free yourself. Do yourself a favor—just say no.

Wiseguys do not carry their money in wallets. They carry their money in big fat rolls.

Wiseguys never, ever take sides against the family. In any situation, the wiseguy is right, the other guy is wrong. Even when a wiseguy is wrong, he's right. Got it?

Wiseguys do not talk about business matters. Instead, they talk about "things." A typical conversation between two mobsters can go for hours without once referring to something specifically. Once I asked Lefty why we were taking a trip to Miami Beach. "Because I wanna see this guy," he explained. "He's gonna introduce me to that guy there who's going to introduce me to the main guy over there." Or a wiseguy might say, "You know that thing we talked about yesterday, that thing with the thing? The guy who is involved with that says we should consider some other things instead." Wiseguys talk around every important business matter. They know that every single word they say might very well be taped. Sometimes it takes investigators months or even years to figure out what the hell wiseguys are talking about on wiretaps.

Wiseguys do not sleep normal hours. Most wiseguys are just getting revved up when the rest of the city is tucking itself in for the night. After dinner most wiseguys will meet at the social club and from there hit the nightspots until two, three in the morning. When you don't have to get up in the morning, what's the point of going to bed early? More time spent cuddling with your wife? Wiseguys are night owls. Wiseguys also know that at any hour of the night, the phone could ring, and they will be expected to get up, get dressed, and report to a designated location. You get a call at four a.m. from your captain telling you to be somewhere—you don't tell him you're tired; you don't check with your wife; you get your ass out of bed and you go. There are no questions to be asked, no: "Why do we have to do it now?" or "Can't it wait until morning?" You just do as you are told, never mind the hour. And if, once you get there, you have to sit around for four or five hours waiting for a capo to leisurely get out of bed to meet you, you sit there and wait. Wiseguys are always at the beck and call of their bosses, day and night.

Wiseguys don't wear a lot of jewelry. Contrary to the image of gangsters created in movies and TV shows, wiseguys do not really favor a lot of jewelry. They don't walk around with thick gold chains around their necks and eight giant rings on their fingers. They like watches—nice, thin, small watches—maybe a Patek Philippe. Maybe they'll wear a thin gold chain with a cross around their neck. Maybe a pinkie ring, not too big. But that's it for the jewelry. It ain't like in the movies, where wiseguys walk around looking like Mr. T.

Wiseguys do not walk around like slobs. Wiseguys always have to be neat. That's another myth created by the movies—that wiseguys spend all their time in dirty, grungy sweatsuits. Wiseguys have a very specific set of rules and codes regarding their appearance that requires they be neat at all times, at least in public. No long hair, no beards, no bushy mustaches—generally, wiseguys will be clean-shaven and shave every day. They get a lot of haircuts because their hair has to be neatly trimmed and styled and combed. In the evenings, they are supposed to wear slacks and a sports coat—a nice, neat sporty look. Suits and ties, of course, when that's appropriate, and the suits have to be neatly pressed and top of the line. Believe it or not, wiseguys are a lot more like Felix than they are like Oscar.

Wiseguys don't forget birthdays. Wiseguys are big on celebrating birthdays and always throw big-deal parties for their capos. One of the most important things a wiseguy has to do is remember his capo's birthday. To forget it is to risk offending and alienating your boss in a way that could prove dangerous down the line. When a capo's birthday rolls around, everybody shows up at the social club and hands the big guy his *aboosta*—an envelope stuffed with at least two hundred dollars and usually much more. Wiseguys also enjoy throwing elaborate parties for their kids and nieces and nephews. Finding the right gift, though, that's another matter. I was with a wiseguy one time, and it was his grandson's birthday, and the kid was going to be seven or eight years old. The wiseguy is deciding what to buy his grandson for his birthday, and he's having a hell of a time figuring out what to get. Finally, he says, "I don't know what I'm going to buy him, but I can't wait until he's eighteen." Why's that, I ask. "Because when he's eighteen I can get him a real birthday present— a machine gun." Happy Birthday, kid—for Christmas, I'll get you the ammo.

Wiseguys don't shake hands. Or at least they don't *just* shake hands, like most business associates do. Wiseguys go the extra mile. The first time wiseguys meet each other or some close associate during the day, they shake hands and kiss each other on both cheeks. That never changes—first meeting, every time, a handshake and two pecks. The next meeting, a simple "Hey, how you doing?" will suffice. But that first meeting—pucker up.

24

WHY YOU CAN'T BULLSHIT A WISEGUY

(Okay, you can, but you got to be good.)

Obviously, it is possible to pull one over on wiseguys. I did it for six years. The wiseguys who were closest to me, who spent twenty hours a day with me for months on end, did not have the first clue that I was anybody but who I said I was: Donnie Brasco, jewel thief. I mean, they were flabber-fucking-gasted when they discovered that I was actually an undercover FBI agent. I wasn't there when they found out, of course, but I can imagine the looks of utter bafflement and disbelief. The gaping mouths and furrowed brows. The FBI agents who showed up at the social club to break the news to Lefty and Sonny had to bring pictures of me with other agents and in FBI offices so that the wiseguys would believe I was a fed. And even when they saw the photos, the wiseguys *still* didn't believe I wasn't a wiseguy. They assumed the FBI agents were working a scam. It took quite a while for the terrible reality to sink in: that is how thoroughly they had the wool pulled over their eyes by the fictional Donnie Brasco.

Of course, what I accomplished while undercover was no fluke—I was good at what I did. Better than good, great. It was a well-planned and well-executed operation, not some fly-by-night deal. I basically had to sacrifice my life and almost my family to do what I did. Even with all that I might have failed, but through a combination of patience, persistence, and really good instincts, I managed to make it work. I pulled one over on some of the most suspicious guys in the world, and that is saying something.

If, however, you come at wiseguys with weaker stuff than I came with, they will eat you alive. They will see right through you, and then they will arrange it so that others can see right through you—by pumping large holes in your body. Wiseguys tend to judge people instantly and pinpoint their weaknesses with amazing accuracy. It is part of their survival mechanism to assess the flaws in other people, in case they need to capitalize on them. Since they are always in this analytical mode, it is difficult to deceive them. If you are trying to bullshit a wiseguy, you had better bring your A-game. Anything less is inviting catastrophe.

Wiseguys, you see, are trained to be suspicious of everything. Their default position is distrust. Until proven otherwise, everyone is a potential threat and a potential target. Most folks, they automatically trust people and give them a lot of leeway before revoking that trust. Most people want to believe that anyone they meet is inherently good and worthy of their time and attention. Not wiseguys. Wiseguys assume you are a scumbag out to rob and harm them. They may let their guard down a little around family members and wiseguys from their crew, but only a little. Wiseguys never completely trust anyone: even those closest to them could turn on a dime and stab them in the heart. That cold, cruel reality of wiseguy life makes it very difficult to dupe a mobster. To be a bad judge of character is a disadvantage in some occupations, but in the Mafia, it is a fatal flaw.

One time, we had this doctor come around our restaurant in Florida and try to sell us some coke. Said he had some drugs that he had access to, and could we move them for him? Coke this, coke that—lots of big talk from this mousy-looking doctor. We figured out the guy was a phony within a few conversations. Probably he was an informant for the Drug Enforcement Agency trying to set us up. The guy continues to come in and jerk us around about all this coke he supposedly had access to.

Finally, me and some other wiseguys go to the guy's office. We want to know when this load of cocaine will arrive. Seeing this guy squirm, it is never more obvious that he doesn't really have access and that the whole thing is probably a setup. Even so, we do a number on his office. Completely trash the place. And we tell him that if he doesn't come up with the cocaine soon, the next thing we trash will be him. After that, the doctor stopped coming around the club.

This guy was taking an extraordinary chance. You do not fuck with wiseguys, especially when it comes to their businesses and their profits. Deceiving wiseguys can be done, but it has to be done just right. Come in with a half-baked plan, you're dead. Get sloppy for just a moment, you're dead. The price of failure is multiple concussions, if you're lucky.

When you think about it, a hair-trigger distrust of everyone is not a bad defense mechanism. No one is saying you have to keep everyone at arm's length, or view the world as a dark, threatening place. But there's no sense in being gullible and pie-in-the-sky, either. Personally, I admire people with trusting spirits, and wide-open hearts, I really do. But I could never be that way. I have seen too much deceit, too much scurrilous behavior, too many truly evil people. Let me get to know you for a while, then I'll decide if I like you. That may sound a little harsh, but what can I say? I've seen the world from a different angle than most people, seen its ugly underbelly up close. When you spend time around wiseguys, you learn that trust is a luxury you really can't afford.

25

WHY WISEGUYS LOVE
DONNIE BRASCO

I **had a half-a-million-dollar contract** on my head. I had wiseguys up and down the East Coast dreaming of blowing my head off. I had one of the mobsters I made look like a monkey staring daggers at me as I sat in the witness box of a federal courtroom, testifying against him. Let's just say it was a pretty tense time.

This particular wiseguy, let's call him Joey, was on trial for racketeering, and I was testifying against him based on the evidence I have collected as Donnie Brasco. In an earlier trial, one of dozens at which I testified after breaking my cover as Donnie, a wiseguy in the gallery looked at me and put his finger to his temple, as if it were a gun. Then he pulled the trigger. I had deceived a lot of wiseguys who counted me as a friend, and now, at their trials, I was turning the final screws and sending them to jail. Making matters worse, my book *Donnie Brasco* had just come out, and in it I basically exposed the stupidity and greediness of mobsters. These wiseguys must have felt like I was rubbing their noses in it.

Certainly Joey, sitting at the defense table, looked like he wanted to twist me into a pretzel. How can I describe Joey? Well, he's fat. Very fat. No other way to put it, a big fat guy. So we break for lunch and I come down off the witness stand and I walk right past Joey, who is sitting at the defendant's table. Sure enough, Joe has something to say to me.

I'm ready for it—what can he say now that means anything? I'll get you, you fucking rat? Yeah, yeah. But still, who likes to have his life threatened under any circumstances. We're talking a stone-cold killer here. So here it comes.

"Hey, Donnie," he says.

"Yeah, Joey?"

"Who you got to play me in the movie?"

The guy's on trial for his life, and his only comment to the guy who's about to put him away is who's going to play him in the movie?

Me, I don't miss a beat.

"You know, Joey, that's the problem. We can't find anyone as fat as you."

That's the thing of it—wiseguys seem to love Donnie Brasco. Not the guy so much as the phenomenon. Wiseguys love movies about wiseguys; they love being depicted on the big screen, and they particularly enjoy being depicted in a glamorous or romantic way. Wiseguys can't get enough of movies about themselves. *The Godfather?* That movie makes wiseguys look like philosophers and noble warriors. Wiseguys know that movie better than most film students.

So it was not surprising to me that wiseguys would love the movie *Donnie Brasco*. Never mind that it shows them in a less than flattering light. It starred Al Pacino as a gangster. What's not to love?

I'm on the set of the movie in Brooklyn one day when I see this guy who looks awfully familiar. I look him over and recognize him as Albie, a wiseguy I knew from the old days. He's hanging around the set, throwing glances at me, just sort of loitering there. I figure, let me get this straightened out right away, find out what the hell is going on. So I go right up to him. If there's going to be trouble, I'm not going to wait for it to come to me.

So I say, "Albie, you need something? Can I help you with something?"

And Albie says, "No, Donnie, I just came by, see what's what." Then he stammers a little. "The thing is, my son wants to be an actor. I'm hoping you can help him out, maybe get him a part as an extra."

There it is. This guy is sworn to hate me and destroy me because I infiltrated the Bonanno family and betrayed the trust of hundreds of wiseguys, but instead he's sucking up to me to get a bit part for his kid. He's playing an angle, and it's all because I've got this major movie coming out. I say, "Albie, are you kidding me? Is this legit?" He tells me his son is a good kid, totally legit, needs a break, all that. Then he says, "Donnie, I got no beef with you, no hard feelings. You never did anything against anyone, never fucked anybody over. Everything you did was on the up and up."

So I meet his kid and he turns out to be a pretty nice kid, and I bring him over to the casting director and tell him to put the kid in the movie somewhere. During the filming, Albie comes to the set every day and brings me some good Cuban cigars. So we sit there in our chairs, me and Albie, reminiscing about the old days, smoking our cigars, having a few laughs. We never talked about business or any of his mob work, although he told me at one point that he was going straight. I knew that was total bullshit—wiseguys don't go straight. Wiseguys stay wiseguys until they die of old age, get murdered, wind up in jail, or enter witness protection. No such thing as retirement to Florida when you're a wiseguy, unless Florida is where they decide to dump your body.

Even so, me and Albie had a nice time of it during the making of *Donnie Brasco*. We did not become friends—like I said, you don't become friends with wiseguys. But we got along pretty good. You would think duping all these wiseguys and then making a movie about it would make me the last person on earth Albie would want to sit and smoke with. Instead, being involved in the movie made me something like a celebrity to these wiseguys. They are suckers for mob movies.

Finally, our movie wraps. When it opens in Philadelphia, a bunch of FBI guys and their wives are lined up outside the theater to see it. While they're waiting in line, they notice all these other guys on line who look pretty familiar. Stocky guys in dark suits. Hey, the feds realize, that's Joey Merlino and his crew. Sure enough, half the Philly mob is on line to see *Donnie Brasco*. The gangsters take their seats in the theater, and the feds decide to sit right behind them, maybe hear a couple of interesting things.

And all through the movie, these wiseguys are making remarks about what a great movie it is.

Who cares what Roger Ebert thinks? My movie got thumbs up from guys who cut off thumbs for a living.

Not every wiseguy, though, was as impressed with me. One time, a lady from Court TV gives me a call and says she wants to do a spot with me in this place down on Mulberry Street. Now, I know this particular place happens to be owned by a capo in a crime family. But, what the hell, I throw on sunglasses and a baseball cap and we go down to this joint to tape the spot.

I walk in, and all these mob guys are sitting there having their linguini and gravy, and a lot of them are looking my way. I know who these guys are, know whose crew each one is part of, but they don't seem to remember me because it's been a few years since I was undercover. So we have a nice dinner and tape a few things, and we go outside to tape one final thing in the street outside the restaurant.

And that's when this one wiseguy comes up to me and says, "You know, you look awful familiar."

"Oh, yeah?" I say. "I guess I have one of those faces."

"I know you," he says.

"Oh, yeah? Well maybe you saw me on TV."

He says, "What are you, an actor?"

I tell him, "Yeah, I'm an actor." Which is not a lie. What was I doing as Donnie Brasco if it wasn't one great fucking acting job?

Then the wiseguy says, "Yeah, maybe that's it. Maybe I saw you on TV. But I definitely know you."

So I say, "Why don't you think about it, and when you figure it out, let me know." And I go over and finish taping my spot on the street, with this wiseguy staring at me and scratching his head, trying to figure out where he knows me from.

He's probably still chewing it over when I leave. Next day, the lady from Court TV calls me up and says, "Boy, did I get a phone call yesterday." Seems the capo who owns the restaurant called her up and let her have it. "How dare you bring that cocksucker Donnie Brasco into my place? That no good rat fucker. In my joint!" She told him she didn't know it was wrong, but I wish she had told him not to worry. I wouldn't be coming back—the mozzarella was no good.

Generally, though, the reaction that wiseguys had to me and to my movie was pretty positive. It's like most of them knew that I was just doing my job, same as them. And then the movie comes out, and it's got Al Pacino and Johnny Depp, and suddenly all any wiseguy can talk about is Donnie Brasco this, Donnie Brasco that.

This other time, I get a call from John Ligato, an FBI agent working undercover in Cleveland. He says, "I got two mob guys coming in from Cleveland, and I'm taking them down to Miami. I need you to meet me and be my Miami contact." Basically, he wants to show these two real gangsters from Cleveland that he has connections to the mob in Miami, and so I'll pretend to be his big wiseguy contact.

It's been years since I assumed the identity of Donnie Brasco. But once in a while I pitch in and help out agents with their undercover assignments. I've been going undercover for twenty years now, and I make a pretty convincing wiseguy. So I become Joe Marino, mobster from Miami.

I go down to Florida, and John and I sit down to lunch with these two fellows from Cleveland. One of them, Richie, starts praising Johnny up and down for bringing in a guy like me who is a tough guy, a real wiseguy, a guy who knows what's going on—one of us. Because, he says, we all have to be careful these days, what with FBI agents trying to crack the mob.

Mind you, four guys are eating lunch at that table, and two of them work for the FBI.

Then Cleveland Richie says, "I'm reading this great book." Oh yeah, I say, what's the book? "*Donnie Brasco*," he says. I say, no kidding? John looks at me and I look at John, and we're wondering if this guy is on to me and just toying with us now. Does he recognize me as the agent who played Donnie Brasco? Is he saying he figured me out by telling me about my own book?

Then he says, "Oh yeah, this is a great book, you got to read it. Because this prick Donnie Brasco was the best undercover agent in FBI history, and by reading this book I'm learning how he was able to infiltrate us." And then he goes on to talk about each chapter—what Donnie did in chapter one, what Donnie pulled off in chapter two, on and on, chapter and verse. This guy knew the book inside out. So I'm there, talking about *Donnie Brasco* with a guy who may or may not know that I *am* Donnie Brasco.

Turns out Richie wasn't on to me at all. In fact, that Christmas, he sent John a present—a hardcover edition of *Donnie Brasco*. I guess Richie never looked too closely at the eight pages of photos inside, some of which pictured me.

That's the thing about going undercover—you become invisible. I ceased to exist as Joe Pistone, but at the same time there was no such person as Donnie Brasco. So who the hell was I? Were these wiseguys going to be mad at Donnie Brasco, who didn't exist, or at Joe Pistone, who they never even met? The character of Donnie Brasco went on to assume a life and celebrity of his own—among wiseguys and among ordinary people.

For instance, my sister-in-law was on a plane once and noticed a lady reading *Donnie Brasco*. My sister-in-law says, "Hey, is that a good book?" The lady says, "Yeah, it's a great book, and not only that, my sister is going out with this guy." Now my sister-in-law knows I'm happily married, but she plays along.

"Oh yeah? Your sister is dating Donnie Brasco?"

The lady goes, "Yeah, he left his wife for her and they're living together in Baltimore."

That's not the first time I heard something like that. What's to stop a guy from saying he's Donnie Brasco? No one knows what I look like, and anyone can read the book and speak with authority about the things I did. And, like I said, Donnie Brasco has assumed a life of his own, way beyond my control. There are probably dozens of Donnie Brascos running around out there, getting laid on my exploits. I say, good luck to them. But they better hope they don't pull that scam on some broad whose uncle is connected.

26

WISEGUYS ALL OVER THE WORLD

My work as an undercover agent has put me in the path of wiseguys from all corners of the globe. Besides your garden-variety American wiseguy, I have dealt with the dangerous Chinese Triads, a scary, ruthless bunch of thugs if ever there was one; the Russian mob, also a particularly lethal and sadistic crew; English wiseguys, as bold and bloody as their American counterparts; and all manner of third world wiseguys. In fact, the closest I ever came to being killed on duty was during an undercover assignment in a third world country.

I should tell you that as Donnie Brasco, I faced death every day. I ran the constant chance that I would be killed in the normal course of operations as a wiseguy: a botched job, an interfamily war, some guy we're shaking down pulls a pistol. I also lived under the constant threat of being exposed as a Special Agent of the FBI. So many different ways my cover could have been blown; so many different times I was a lie or two away from being found out. I look back now, and I think that I was extraordinarily lucky to have made it through that assignment alive. Either that, or I was incredibly good.

Certainly I understood the risks going in. Undercover operations are a particularly hazardous line of work. You have no way of knowing if you've been made or if the next guy through the door is going to blow your cover—or blow your brains out. If you're going to be an undercover agent, you have to learn to not think about the risks involved. The key is keeping your cool in the most stressful of circumstances. Plenty of times as Donnie Brasco, my heart was beating a mile a minute or my insides were churning like crazy. But I never lost my cool, not for a moment. That is what kept me alive.

I have come close to being killed many times as an FBI agent, and I have found a way to cheat that nasty fate every time. Sometimes it has gone down to the wire. That was the case in this third world country, where I went to work as an undercover agent long after I had retired Donnie Brasco.

For security reasons, I cannot tell you the name of the country. Nor can I tell you what, precisely, my mission was. I can say that this particular third world country was overrun by unsavory individuals who were trying to make it a haven for drug smugglers, a drop-off point for massive amounts of drugs on their way to other countries, including the U.S. I went in undercover with another agent, let's call him Chuck, and our mission was to deal with these drug thugs and, if possible, get them to leave the country. Only one person in the entire country would know who Chuck and I really were, and that was a colonel in the country's army. Everyone else, including the thugs, believed we were two wiseguys from America interested in their business.

It's one thing dealing with wiseguys in your native country. It's another dealing with drug-running thugs in a third world country. Wiseguys weren't going to pull out a gun and shoot you in the head on a whim. There was, with wiseguys, at least a modicum of respect for the sanctity of life. With these drug runners, I could not be sure of anything. Chuck and I knew our margin for error was nonexistent.

We flew into the country and through our contacts arranged a meeting with the head gangster. Our job was to sit him down and explain to him, through any means necessary, the wisdom of his pulling up stakes and leaving the country. We knew that, with millions of dollars on the line, it would not be an easy sell. So we get into our rented Jeep and drive up into the mountains, to this gangster's secluded compound. Some low-level guys escort us in and we meet with this chief in his big dining room. We say what we have to say, and we get it over with quick. Everything goes smoothly; everyone is pleasant. We are escorted out, we get back in our Jeep, and we drive down the mountain, happy to be done with this guy.

We go back to our nice hotel, where Chuck and I have adjoining suites. We keep the door between our rooms open all the time, just in case. We've been in the country three or four days now, and this is our last night. We both feel pretty good that we have done what we came to do, and that now we get to leave this sorry little country. Chuck finishes dressing before I do, and says he will meet me in the hotel restaurant. He is gone about ten minutes when the telephone rings.

"Room service," the man on the line says. I say I didn't order any room service. The man hangs up and I continue getting dressed.

A couple of minutes later, the phone rings again. And again the guy says, "Room service." What the fuck is this, I think. I didn't order any room service. I hang up again, and now I'm kind of suspicious. We're on the second floor of the hotel, so I know I can jump off the balcony if I need to. Also, I have a pearl-handled .45 caliber gun that the army colonel has given me. Still, I think that maybe it's time I finish getting dressed and go meet Chuck in the restaurant.

Then there is a knock at the door. "Room service," I hear the guy say.

Through the closed door I tell the guy I didn't order room service. I've got my gun in my hand, and I gently put my ear to the door. I hear voices out there, squabbling about something. Right away, I know something is wrong: it doesn't take more than one person to deliver room service. I figure my shot is jumping off the balcony and getting the fuck out of here. So I peek out the curtains and see two guys standing just below my room.

Both guys are holding submachine guns.

And then there's another knock at the door.

"Who is it?" I say. "Room service, room service." What the fuck am I going to do now, I think. I figure the only thing I can do is open the front door. I still have to think that I am not going to get shot for no good reason. Then I think I better put my gun away. If I open the door and they see I am armed, they are likely to start firing. I tuck my gun under the mattress and open the door. As soon as it's open a crack, five guys barge in and knock me to the ground.

Then they start pistol-whipping me.

I'm on the floor fighting these guys off, trying to get to my feet. They are hitting me with their pistols and kicking me all over. Finally, they subdue me and cuff my hands behind my back. One of the guys, the lead guy, walks over to a travel bag I have hanging on the back of my closet door. I can see clearly that in his hand he is holding a plastic bag filled with something that resembles cocaine. He approaches my travel bag and comes back from the closet, and now the bag he was holding is gone. "What the fuck are you doing?" I say. "Nothing, nothing," he says in his broken English. "What the fuck did you just put in my bag?" I say. The guy responds by smack-ing me in the face with his gun. The metallic taste of blood fills my mouth.

I'm a little woozy when one of the other guys goes over to my travel bag and pulls out a bag of coke. The lead thug says, "Oh, I see, you're a drug dealer, an assassin." I say, "I don't know what the fuck you're talking about."

"Where is you partner?" he demands.

"What partner? I don't know what the fuck you're talking about."

"The guy in the next room," they say. "Where is he?"

"I don't know whose fucking room that is," I say. "That room has nothing to do with me."

They are irritated now, and they work me over some more. A couple of them hit me with their pistols, a couple of the other guys slap me around with their fists. My hands are cuffed behind my back so I can do nothing to stop them.

"Where is your partner?" they keep asking.

"I'm just here on vacation," I keep telling them.

"No, you are a drug dealer, an assassin. You are here to assassinate our president."

Now it's been about an hour since Chuck left, and he must be wondering where the fuck I am. I am hoping these guys are done with me before Chuck wanders back to the room to find me. But I know that Chuck is not going to sit downstairs forever. Sure enough, he pops his head into my room. The five guys grab him up, and now the two of us are cuffed and totally at their mercy. The goons march us out of the hotel and throw us into the back of a Jeep. From the markings on the Jeep I can tell these lowlife thugs are part of the local police force.

It's after midnight when we drive up to the police station, which is actually a beat-up old barracks. They drag us up to the police captain, with his typical fat fucking belly and big fat cigar. This would almost be comical if it weren't deadly serious. By now, I am starting to lose feeling in my left hand, because the cuffs are on too tight. Several times I ask the thugs to loosen my cuffs, and every time they ignore me. Until the last time, when one of the thugs tightens my cuffs.

The interrogation continues. "You are drug dealers, assassins"—all that shit.

"I don't know what the fuck you're talking about; we're tourists down for a couple of days of vacation." They aren't buying this, primarily because they tossed my hotel room and found my gun. Now they are sure we are assassins. They keep harassing us and asking us questions for the next two, three hours. It feels like all feeling in my hands is gone.

Then things get really interesting. Because they can't get anything out of us this way, they march me out of the police station and up the stairs of an adjacent building. We go up to the fifth, maybe the sixth floor. They push me into a room and keep asking me questions about who I am. They push me out onto a balcony and ask more questions. Chuck and I keep saying we don't know anything.

Then two of the thugs grab me by my belt and hoist me over the fucking railing.

I look down and I see the pavement way, way below me. You might think I was scared shitless at this point, but the truth is I was not. Was I upset? Sure. Uncomfortable? Yeah. They got me by the belt and they are dangling me off the sixth floor and telling me they're going to drop me if I don't tell them the truth. Wouldn't you be a little out of sorts? But I had been trained to keep my cool in adverse situations, and because of this training, coupled with my experience undercover in the Bonanno crime family, the more adverse the situation got, the less likely I was to lose my cool. I knew that the key to surviving was maintaining my composure at all costs. Under no circumstances do you ever allow your tormentor to see that he has broken your spirit. Once he knows he has the power to scare you out of your wits, he pretty much has the green light to do anything he wants to you. But if he sees that even dangling you over a balcony railing isn't enough to rattle you, then he has to think twice about what his next move will be. Still, you think to yourself, hanging upside-down several floors above the pavement would frighten even the toughest of customers. Not true. Training and experience allow me to block out the obvious peril of the situation and focus on reacting in a way that will gain me some advantage. Keeping my cool as I dangle from the balcony assures me of having the wherewithal to formulate a plan. I resort to one of my best weapons as an undercover agent. Plain and simple, I bluff. Big time.

"I got nothing to fucking tell you," I say, "so if you're going to fucking drop me, you better fucking drop me and get it over with."

Hanging over that railing was probably the closest I ever came to dying. Until the next few minutes.

Finally, these lowlife goons figure I have nothing to tell them, so they pull me back onto the balcony. They push me into the room, where I see Chuck. The thugs start speaking in their native tongue, making some sort of plan. Luckily for us, Chuck speaks the language. Chuck draws close to me and whispers what he hears: these guys are going to take us out to the jungle and shoot us and leave us there, so no one will ever find our bodies.

This is what you call the moment of truth. Whatever play we have, we better play it now. We cannot allow ourselves to be taken to that jungle. We have only one shot, and it is a dicey shot at that. We decide to invoke the name of the colonel.

This could go two ways. If these thugs are political enemies of the colonel, then the last thing they'll want to do is let him know they rounded up a couple of his friends and tortured them for five hours. If this is the case, invoking the colonel's name will get us shot and dumped in the jungle for sure. If, however, they are on the same side as the colonel, they can explain why they grabbed us up and maybe squirm out of it. If they are the colonel's friends, we have a shot.

They are just about to drag us out of the room when Chuck asks them if they know the colonel.

This stops them in their tracks.

I try to read their faces, to see where we stand. The fat police captain says, yes, we know the colonel. What of it? Chuck says, "Yeah, well, we know that colonel too, so you better give him a call at his home before you do anything to us." Now the fat police captain is shitting his pants. He doesn't want to call the colonel at five in the morning, wake him up out of a dead sleep. But we remind him that before he does anything to us, he better check with the colonel first. If he wants to wait, that's fine with us. Just check with the colonel first.

Finally, the police captain makes the call. We watch as his face goes green. Within a few minutes, we are driven back to the hotel and our cuffs are taken off. I look around for the guy who tightened my cuffs, and when I find him, I hit him as hard as I can in the face. Then I beat the shit out of him, and I tell him why I am beating the shit out of him. The other goons stand around and watch.

Later that day, we meet with the colonel, and he makes sure we have safe passage out of the country. We get out with our lives, and all because we kept our cool. If you don't have the stomach for really close calls, then stay the fuck away from undercover work.

27

WISEGUYS ARE PATRIOTIC

You might think a group of people who devote their lives to breaking the law would not be particularly patriotic citizens. But the fact is, wiseguys are very pro-America. Despite their deep roots in Italy, this country's blood enemy in World War II, and despite their blatant disregard for the rules and boundaries of civilized American society, wiseguys are emphatically patriotic types. You will always hear them talking about what a wonderful country this is. The reason is simple. Where else but in this great, freedom-loving country could they get away with as much shit as they do?

Which is not to say that wiseguys are steeped in American history, or even all that up on its major holidays. One day while I was sitting around a social club with a bunch of wiseguys, just a few days before the Fourth of July, one gangster who was especially slow on the uptake piped up and asked, "When's the Fourth of July due?" Naturally, I explained to him that, this year, the Fourth of July fell on August fifteenth.

WISEGUYS ARE CHEAP

Wiseguys like living high on the hog. The wear the best clothes, eat at the best restaurants, drink the best booze, sleep with the best hookers. If you look at their lifestyle, you might deduce that they are spending all of their profits on living the good life. Not true. Wiseguys are notoriously cheap. They are only big spenders when they are spending someone else's money.

Start with the suits. Sure, they only wear tailored suits that cost two, three thousand dollars. But you can be sure they didn't pay retail or even wholesale for the threads. They were either given the clothing by the manufacturer as part of a payoff, or the suits are swag—stolen merchandise. Every nice piece of clothing on a gangster is almost definitely swag—the suits, the shirts, the ties, the shoes, even the cuff links. The whole fucking ensemble fell off the back of a truck. Very seldom does a wiseguy spend his own money to buy himself a fancy suit. They just don't part with their money that easily.

So what about the pricey booze? Stolen. The Courvoisier in the back of the social club? Swag. And the expensive meals at four-star restaurants? Comped. When wiseguys go out, everything is on the arm—given to them for free. Maybe the owner of the restaurant knows who they are and is smart enough to swallow the tab to keep his local wiseguys happy. Maybe the meals are part of an extorted protection deal. Maybe the restaurant is run by someone who is connected. Whatever the arrangement, the check never comes. Heaping plates of immaculately prepared pasta are lavished on their table as if the wiseguys were food critics from the *New York Times*, and they won't pay for a single fucking noodle. When gangsters go out, everything is on the arm. Call it the wiseguy's welfare.

And it's not like wiseguys just get lucky and stumble into places where the waiters and owners take care of them. Wiseguys are *always* looking for something on the arm. They will go out of their way to eat at friendly restaurants, rather than pay full freight at places across the street. That's because, for all their wads of cash as thick as rolls of toilet paper, wiseguys hate peeling off as much as a dollar bill. Paying your own way is for suckers. Wiseguys never pick up the check.

29

WISEGUYS AREN'T GREAT SHOTS

When it comes to killing people, wiseguys do much better at close range. Percentage-wise, they are close to one hundred percent when the method of execution is two to the back of the head. Sneaking up behind someone and blowing their brains out is an incredibly effective method of ending someone's life, and thus, the wiseguy's preferred method of murder. However, you cannot always get that close to your target. Sometimes, wiseguys have to be good marksmen. When they are called upon to fire from a distance, the percentages drop dramatically.

The botched hit is a common occurrence in the world of the wiseguy. Happens all the time. You'd think these guys would be experts already, given that murder is such a routine part of their business. But sometimes they seem like amateurs. And I'm not just talking about bad marksmanship. This one time, a couple of wiseguys got the contract to kill this other guy they didn't know. Usually you know the person you are assigned to kill, but once in a while, all you have to work with is a name, not even a photo. So they got this guy's address and they started following him around for a few days, figuring out his comings and goings. Finally, they decide on the best time and place to kill him. They get ready to do it, but just an hour or two before the designated time, one of the wiseguys decides to double-check that they have the right guy. Turns out they didn't—they got the wrong address right off the bat. This poor bastard came within a couple of hours to getting killed for no good reason. We're not talking about geniuses here.

Even when wiseguys have the right guy, things can go terribly wrong. Killing someone, it turns out, is not as easy as it looks on TV. Mob boss Joseph "Skinny Joe" Merlino survived not one, not two, but nearly two *dozen* assassination attempts. One time, rival mobster John Stanfa sent a capo to drive past Merlino's clubhouse, where they found Merlino and an associate walking down the street. They opened fire, killing the associate, but Merlino was merely wounded in the ass.

Ironically, the capo who botched that hit, John Veasey, survived an attempt on his own life one year later. Wiseguys had him sitting in a chair in his apartment with a gun pointed at his head—and they *still* could not kill him. They shot Veasey several times, beat him with their guns, pushed him down a flight of stairs, and tried to slash his throat. Veasey got away and lived to tell the tale.

The late Salvatore "Salvie" Testa cheated death an amazing seventeen times. Salvy was himself an expert killer who murdered everyone involved in the legendary hit on his father, Chicken Man Testa. In the process he made a lot of enemies but survived attempt after attempt on his life. Not surprisingly, he was allegedly set up by his best friend and finally killed at age twenty-eight. The method: two shots to the back of the head, at close range.

30

WISEGUYS LOVE THEIR FOOD

*T**he Sopranos* **gets at least one thing right:** they always show Tony Soprano stuffing his face. Every show, he's eating in at least four or five scenes. That is absolutely true to life. Wiseguys love to eat.

Wiseguys eat several meals a day. Maybe you start with coffee and a roll, but then you maybe have another breakfast at home or at the club. You also eat a big lunch at the club, then go home for dinner with the family. Then you eat another dinner when you meet up with the wiseguys at night. And if there's a meeting with other wiseguys or bosses, that's another meal right there. There is no telling how many meals a wiseguy will eat in a day. And we're not talking snacks, either. We're talking full-blown, five-course meals.

Wiseguys have turned food preparation into a fetish. Remember the scene in *Goodfellas* where Paul Sorvino is lovingly cutting the pepperoni into slices as thin as a stamp? You see that stuff all the time. Wiseguys obsess about food. What kinds of food? Well, pasta, of course. Ziti, linguini, shells, ravioli, usually cooked al dente. Sauce, heaps and heaps of sauce, made from fresh tomatoes and spiced just right. It is a badge of honor to be a wiseguy who is known for preparing a good tomato sauce. Meatballs, of course, the size of pool balls. Sausage and peppers. Broccoli rabe. Braciole. Fish, chicken, steaks, chops. Calamari is popular, fresh, not fried. Breads must also be fresh. Cheeses, they love: a good mozzarella, soft and juicy, is to wiseguys what blood is to Dracula. Then they wash everything down with an expensive Italian wine and a good cup of espresso.

Since food is so important to wiseguys, the best way to insult them, short of disparaging their wives or mothers, is to crack wise about what they serve you. I remember going undercover to try and get at the wiseguy who owned a restaurant in Miami. This other undercover agent brought me in, and I was supposed to be the guy's big New York mob connection. So we're in this wiseguy's restaurant, and he's trying to act like a real tough guy, and he's going on about how nobody's moving into his territory without his permission and this and that. It is early in the meal, so we let it go.

So we're sitting in his restaurant, and he's having the chef bring out these big plates of food—showing off for us. Big, groaning plates of calamari, shrimp, meatballs, salads. We're all eating and drinking wine and talking about our businesses, and then the discussion gets pretty heavy. The guy starts again with how nobody is going to move into his territory without cutting him in on any profits from gambling or loan-sharking or drugs or whatever. This guy knows who I am, knows I'm supposed to be a big wiseguy from New York, but he's making a play, trying to intimidate me. Finally, I say, "Listen, we don't need any permission from you to come down here and do what we're going to do, you know? We'll cut you in out of the goodness of our hearts and give you what we think is fair." And it's like the guy didn't hear a word I said. He keeps up with his threats and says, "Anybody that comes here and cuts into my territory, they are liable to die over it."

Okay, that's it. I push my chair back, get up and say, "The only thing people are going to die from is the fucking food in your fucking restaurant 'cause it's shit. Worst fucking food I ever tasted." And with that I storm out of the place.

Needless to say, we didn't have any trouble with that wiseguy after that.

31

HOW WISEGUYS GO
TO THE MATTRESSES

Wiseguys do not live in a perpetual state of conflict with other families. Most of the time, things are peaceful and wiseguys go happily about their various scams and rackets. But, once in a while, something triggers a war between crime families. That's when wiseguys go to the mattresses.

"Going to the mattresses" means going to war. It is the term wiseguys use to signify a high state of alert. Basically, everything changes for a wiseguy when an interfamily war is triggered. Maybe a rival boss is whacked in a power play. Maybe one family fucks another over in a big deal. Whatever the reason, every few years rival families go to war. The word gets out, and wiseguys know just what to do.

First thing a wiseguy does is pack his piece. Normally, wiseguys do not walk around with their guns in their belts. It's uncomfortable, after all, to have a hunk of metal stuck in your waist, particularly if you're a fat fuck. But when there is a war, you carry your piece at all times.

Next, you abandon all your regular routines and stay away from your familiar haunts. When there is a shooting war, all the wiseguys from a particular crew come together and literally live with each other, round the clock. You live out of the social club or some apartment in the neighborhood, and you sleep on spare beds on the floor—hence, going to the mattresses. The idea is to keep the wiseguys together, lessening the chances that they will be picked off one by one.

So now you have a roomful of wiseguys living together like a fucking sleepaway camp. One guy is selected to be the cook, and you stock up on enough food and groceries to keep you going for days or even weeks. You can make phone calls and bring people around and do whatever you have to do to keep your normal businesses going. Most of your time is spent hanging out, playing cards, bullshitting, just like you do at the club. But during a shooting war you do not leave at the end of the day. Forget your wife, your mistress, your other mistress. You stay and wait for runners to come by and give you news about what's going on. At some point, the crew might be summoned to show up somewhere and throw down. Or maybe that call never comes. Eventually, the runner comes around and says peace has been negotiated and the war is over. The mattresses are put away, the guns put back in the drawers. Now you can go back to doing what you ordinarily do—hanging out, playing cards, bullshitting.

32

WISEGUYS HAVE
NO FRIENDS

Wiseguys spend twenty hours a day with each other, play pool and deal cards with each other, go to each other's weddings and kids' birthdays, hug and kiss each other like great friends. But they are not friends. Wiseguys have no friends. Being someone's friend means trusting them and sharing your deepest thoughts and fears with them. In the Mafia, you cannot afford to be that vulnerable. You cannot afford to have friends.

Naturally, wiseguys grow close to each other. I certainly shared some laughs and had some fun with the wiseguys I knew. But I never, not for a moment, thought of them as friends, not just because I was FBI and they were wiseguys, but because wiseguys themselves do not think of each other as friends. They are friendly, but not friends. The term "friend" has no meaning when, at any time, you may be asked to blow the head off a guy you've known and liked for years.

Friends are good for one thing in the mob: they can be counted on to kill you when your number comes up. One of the first things Lefty taught me is that the guy who kills you will most likely be the guy who's closest to you. I knew that if my cover got blown and the orders came down to kill me, it would be Lefty who pulled the trigger. A couple of times, when he walked behind me in a dark alley or a deserted dock, I couldn't help but think: is this it? You know this about the wiseguys you are friendly with, but it does not make you want to spend any less time with them. You might be asked to kill them, they may be asked to kill you, what are you going to do? That's life in the mob.

So it is that wiseguys are actually pretty lonely guys. When they're with their families, they want to be with their girlfriends. When they're with their girlfriends, they want to be with their other girlfriends. When they're with their other girlfriends, they want to be with other wiseguys. And when they're with other wiseguys, they have to worry about getting whacked. Wiseguys don't make deep connections. They share nothing with nobody, open up to absolutely no one, spend most of their time with people they happily scam, cheat, or kill. In other lines of work, they might be great guys to hang out with, get to know, become friends with. But they have chosen a very strange and unnatural line of work. They are wiseguys, and wiseguys can trust only themselves. If you want to make friends, join a country club. If you want to make money, join the mob.

33

OLD WISEGUYS,
NEW WISEGUYS

By the time I joined the Bonanno family as Donnie Brasco, the Mafia was beginning to decline in power and influence. In my years undercover, it would decline even more. There is no question that several different factors combined to deal a damaging blow to organized crime. Like I said earlier, the Mafia was not crippled or wiped out in any way. It exists today and most surely will exist for years or even decades to come. But it is also true that the Mafia today is not nearly as big and powerful and untouchable as it was in years past.

For starters, the Mafia was diminished by the aggressive tactics of the federal government in its war with the mob. Starting in the late 1960s and on through the 1980s, the feds picked up one incredible weapon after another—the ability to plant bugs in the homes and social clubs of gangsters and produce thousands of hours of wiretaps; the 1970 RICO act, which allowed prosecutors to lasso mobsters with the catchall charge of racketeering; the advent of the witness protection program, which gave gangsters a cushy place to fall after they flipped; and a general determination by dogged federal agents—guys like Rudy Giuliani—to not shy away from going after mobsters. In the old days, wiseguys were very tough to catch in the act and successfully prosecute, but that all changed when these weapons began to be deployed. In 1985, the feds arrested and indicted the bosses of all five of New York's crime families, an unprecedented and brazen move by previously skittish government prosecutors. Castellano, Persico, Corallo, Rastelli and Salerno—all rounded up and cuffed under RICO statutes. After countless hours of testimony—some from yours truly—all the defendants in the final case were found guilty. Sure, new bosses stepped up to keep the five families running. But it was more apparent than ever that mobsters were vulnerable, and that continues to be the case today.

Aggressive tactics by the feds, however, is only one reason why the Mafia has lost some of its luster. It has also seen a passing of the torch from an older generation of mobsters to a new breed of wiseguy. This has not been a positive change for the mob. The old generation believed in and adhered to the traditions and customs and codes of the Mafia as they were handed down by the Sicilians. These wiseguys weren't far removed from the people who founded the Mafia in the late 1800s, and they believed with all their hearts in the principles of *la cosa nostra*. They literally lived and died by the rules laid out by the founders. These rules worked pretty well for them, and they trusted in them completely.

But as the years passed, and the old wiseguys died out, and the new blood came in, this devotion to the traditional way of doing things slackened. Now you had wiseguys with no sense of the history of the Mafia or of its customs and traditions. The organized part of organized crime became just a shadow of what it was, with disastrous results. The embodiment of the new and reckless breed of wiseguy is, of course, John Gotti.

Gotti disregarded Mafia customs when he had Paul Castellano whacked without the approval of the Commission. But that was nothing compared to what he did once he became boss. Basically, he made his family a giant target for prosecutors and drew more negative attention to the mob than perhaps any wiseguy in history.

Gotti's crime was believing his own press clippings. He loved to read about himself in the newspaper, and the more reporters referred to him as the Dapper Don, the more he put himself out there for public scrutiny. He would show up for court hearings in his fancy double-breasted suits, strutting like a peacock and ticking off the feds. This was a drastic change from the way old wiseguys conducted business. In the old days, a wiseguy did everything in the shadows, under the radar, away from the limelight. But Gotti liked to set off fireworks in Ozone Park, hang out in front of his Little Italy social club, and generally act like some kind of celebrity. Lots of bosses in the old days were known around town, but they always insisted they were legitimate businessmen. Gotti did not try to hide the fact that he was a wiseguy; in fact, it was the source of the fame he so craved. Essentially, he invited the government to come and get him, which is just what it did. Sure, he slipped away a couple of times on technicalities, but eventually Gotti was convicted, and he died in jail. Gotti's legacy is that his ego and vanity led him to unnecessarily expose the mob to the attention of investigators, who seized this chance to deal a crippling blow to the Gambino crime family.

The recklessness of the new wiseguy is also apparent in his approach to the business of drugs. A lot of times you'll hear that old-time wiseguys did not want to be involved with drugs. That narcotics were a big no-no. Fact is, the old-timers were involved in importing and distributing drugs. There was simply too much money at stake for them to keep their hands clean. But they did take a dismal view of drugs and people who used drugs, and they handled this business carefully. For instance, they made sure to keep narcotics out of their neighborhoods, and certainly they did not use drugs themselves. There was a certain orderliness to the mob drug trade. Today, that caution is out the fucking window. The new wiseguys are far more interested in the money they can make off drugs than they are in keeping it out of their neighborhoods or even their own bodies. Lots of wiseguys become addicts and get careless and sloppy. Coke, weed, heroin—you name it, I've seen wiseguys do it. These are guys who basically have no respect for the old way of doing things, for the traditions and customs that had kept the Mafia in business for a century. Instead, they believe in instant gratification, making as much money as they can, plying their drugs in previously nice neighborhoods and basically acting like common crooks. All of this is a major difference from the way things used to be before I came on board.

What we're talking about here is a new breed of wiseguy who is neither as smart nor as forward-thinking as his predecessors. Today's wiseguy is a lot more careless and stupid and sloppy than the old-time gangsters. As a result, a lot of the strengths of the old Mafia have been squandered and lost.

For instance, the Mafia has more or less lost its stranglehold on the unions. A lot of this is because of the aggressiveness of federal agents, but a lot of it is because new wiseguys do not have the smarts and wherewithal to cultivate the union people like the old wiseguys did. Garbage carting, the loading docks, the garment industry— wiseguys used to absolutely own these enterprises. That's because the old wiseguys knew how to handle union bosses, knew how to schmooze them, and bring them into the fold, and corrupt them, and keep them happy. They knew that if you controlled the unions, you controlled the fucking country. They would have frequent sit-downs with the unions, with politicians, with all sorts of officials, and they would negotiate deals and arrangements that insured they kept control of hundreds of locals. This approach worked beautifully for decades, fueled by money and the mutual greed of all participants. Today, the mob no longer has a death grip on the unions, and as a result, its reach and power are diminished.

Put simply, new wiseguys are not bound by the time-tested traditions and rules of conduct that governed the mob for years, and nowhere is this more evident than in the disregard today's wiseguys have for the code of *omerta*—the vow of silence. If John Gotti embodied the reckless and stupidity of the new wiseguy, then his underboss, Salvatore Gravano, embodies the new wiseguy's disposition to put himself above the family and squeal to the feds. Basically, you have more wiseguys turning stool pigeon in the last ten or twenty years than in all the previous decades of the Mafia's history. Forget about the fact that electronic surveillance has given feds access to damning testimony that they would never have had access to in the old days. The real problem is wiseguys opting to betray their crime families and go into witness protection rather than spend a single day in jail. Old wiseguys would get pinched, bite the bullet, button their lips, and do their time. Today, the first thing a wiseguy does is sing.

None sang as magnificently as Sammy "The Bull" Gravano. Gotti's murderous right-hand man—he admitted to whacking at least nineteen guys—Gravano got arrested along with his boss in 1990. When feds played a tape for him of Gotti blaming some murders on him, Gravano flipped like a seal at Sea World. He not only told prosecutors all about the Castellano killing and a bunch of other murders, he took the stand against his old boss and delivered nine days of incredibly incriminating testimony. He helped put Gotti and dozens of other gangsters in jail. It was the most thorough and damaging betrayal of the Mafia by a wiseguy that had ever occurred. Gravano got sent into a cushy exile in Arizona, but, true to form, began dealing drugs and got arrested all over again. By then, he had already proven beyond any doubt that the code of *omerta* was as dead and buried as the nineteen guys he killed.

So there you have them, Gotti and Gravano—poster boys for the new wiseguy. As a former federal agent, I can tell you that we were all delighted that wiseguys became more careless and stupid, and less respectful of the mob's trusted rules of conduct. Believe me, we needed all the help we could get to win some key victories in our war against the mob. But students of the Mafia may be saddened that today's wiseguy is such a pale copy of his predecessors. Where is the cunning, the guile, the incredible survival instincts? Fughedaboudit. One modern wiseguy tattooed messages of revenge on his body, making it easier for a jury to link him to his victims. Al Capone, these guys ain't.

34

THE WAY OF
THE WISEGUY

Lefty takes me down to Miami to talk to some crooked Cuban bankers about getting involved in the cocaine trade. I sit quietly in this one banker's office while Lefty does the talking. All of a sudden the banker starts pretending like he isn't involved in drugs and wants nothing to do with us. I mean, he completely changed his tune in the course of our brief conversation with him. Finally, Lefty and I took off, baffled by what it was that had scared this guy. I assumed that Lefty had come on too strong.

In fact, the guy had been spooked by me. "I look into those eyes of Donnie and they're killer eyes," an intermediary later told us the banker admitted. "I don't want to have anything to do with that Donnie." Lefty had killed all sorts of people and here this banker is scared of an FBI agent.

But the truth is, in that banker's office, I was every bit the wiseguy. I had to be—if I was anything less than one hundred percent authentic in my portrayal of a gangster, I would have been killed. In the early days as Donnie Brasco, I made a pretty convincing thief and street guy—convincing enough to blend in with some heavy hitters in the Bonanno family. But it was only after spending months and months with Lefty Ruggiero that I really learned what it means to be a mobster—that I truly picked up the way of the wiseguy.

Lefty took me under his wing and taught me everything a good wiseguy needs to know. Little things—how to look, how to listen, when to speak, when to shut up. The protocol of surviving a life of crime. Like I said, there is nothing admirable about wiseguys, and I am not saying I learned valuable lessons from them. All I'm saying is that I got this rare opportunity to explore a lifestyle few people ever get to see, and what I saw was human nature stripped bare of the civility and inhibitions that govern the rest of us.

I knew about a lot of this stuff before I ever hooked up with Lefty and even before I became a Special Agent of the FBI. I grew up on the streets of an Italian neighborhood, and I hung around with wiseguy types all the time. I played in some card games that I knew were run by mob guys, and I spent time in social clubs that I knew were home to gangsters. I learned the basics of this kind of life—hustling for scores, keeping your mouth shut, not getting involved in matters that didn't concern you. Had I been so inclined, I could have joined the Mafia long before it occurred to me to join the FBI. But I had a couple of good hardworking parents who instilled in me a pretty solid work ethic. I went the other way.

Even so, growing up on the streets and around wiseguys gave me a different view of them than the one held by many law enforcement officers. I did not see them as especially evil or loathsome; to me, they were just guys who grew up in a particular culture and under particular economic conditions and chose to become wiseguys, like other guys choose to become bakers or businessmen. I had no great score to settle with them when I joined the FBI. Neither did I have any inclination to cut them slack. I knew who they were, understood how they thought, and when it became my job to help put them behind bars, I did it like anybody does a job they take seriously.

When I went undercover as Donnie Brasco, my education in the way of the wiseguy began in earnest. I was no longer hanging around wiseguys—I *was* a wiseguy. I never forgot who I was or what I was fighting to achieve, but I did allow certain parts of my personality to be subsumed and replaced by wiseguy traits. I had to expose myself to the full sweep of wiseguy wickedness. Violence, greed, manipulation, exploitation—these are the raw impulses that define life as a wiseguy. They walk the same streets as us but by no means are they seeing or feeling the same things.

That was one of the most amazing things Lefty taught me—how to look at things like a wiseguy. It was like wearing X-ray glasses. One time Lefty schooled me in how to case a bar—who is sitting where, who is nursing what drink, who talks too much to the bartender, who might be a guy we could do business with down the road. These were things that nobody but a wiseguy would notice in a million years. They had to play every angle they could just to keep up in their world. Not only that, but they had to do this all the fucking time. Sure, everybody has to hustle at their jobs to win a promotion or a raise. Wiseguys have to hustle to keep their earnings up so they don't get whacked. They never, ever stop scamming and scheming. I remember once Lefty caught his son watching *All My Children*. "Turn off them fucking soap boxes!" he yelled. "You should be out stealing." Talk about instilling a work ethic.

As a wiseguy, I was forced to live on the edge. I had to become accustomed to the constant threat of being killed. In fact, I was under twice the pressure faced by real wiseguys. If they fucked up or showed disrespect, sure, they got whacked. Such a fate could have easily befallen me. But on top of that, I could have had my cover broken and been revealed as an FBI agent. One slip-up, one lie I forgot I told, and I could have been shot on the spot. This up-close-and-personal relationship with your own mortality is something most people cannot even fathom, but wiseguys shrug it off like dandruff. All wiseguys fully expect to either go to jail or get whacked. They have absolutely no delusions that they are going to live long lives and bounce their grandkids on their knees. Of course, many of them do live long lives and bounce their grandkids on their knees. Somehow, either through cunning or incredible luck, they manage to avoid getting whacked or serving fifty in the slammer, and they move down to Florida to grow old and eat early dinners. Joe Bonanno was something like ninety-seven fucking years old when he finally died. But no wiseguy *expects* to reach that ripe old age. They expect to do hard time or die in a back alley. Is the death rate higher for wiseguys than it is for, say, sanitation workers? Sure. Sanitation workers don't get guns pressed against the back of their heads in parking garages as a consequence of not doing their jobs properly. But wiseguys know they are entering a dangerous profession when they sign up. The reality of getting whacked is so omnipresent that it finally ends up not being a factor at all. You have no choice but to ignore it, because dwelling on it would make you a jittery mess. To this day I walk around with a five-hundred-thousand-dollar price on my head. Do I dwell on it? No. Am I ready? You bet. Death is just a fact of life for wiseguys, and they are far more prepared for that eventuality than most people. You might even say that in their approach to their own mortality, wiseguys are pretty enlightened, even zen. Wasn't it Buddha who said, "Hey, when you're number's up, it's up; fughedaboudit."?

It was all part of my six-year course at Wiseguy University, an education that I have tried to share with law enforcement officers at every turn. I think the things I learned about wiseguys have and will continue to help in the war against the mob. But I also know that many of the things I experienced cannot be transferred to anyone else in the course of a lecture or in a book. You just had to be there.

So what do I expect you, the reader, to get out of this book? What's in it for you, now that you know about the way of the wiseguy? Maybe a little insight into the darker side of human nature, into the crazy impulses we all manage to control but that wiseguys let run wild. Maybe a little better understanding of a rich part of this country's history. Maybe nothing. Like I said, I'm not here to push any lessons on anybody.

Me, I came through my time undercover pretty much unscathed. I know that's hard for some people to believe, but it's true. How could I have spent six years around these wiseguys— around all that thieving and conniving and murdering—and not have been permanently affected? Hey, it's not like I came from some lily-white background and suddenly found myself inside a seedy social club. I knew who I was going in, and I was the same guy coming out. Same values, same beliefs, same guy.

The one thing that did stick with me long after I ceased being Donnie Brasco was the wiseguy attitude. Not backing down from confrontations, standing up for yourself, taking no shit, cutting corners here and there. I'm not talking about acting like a tough guy or throwing your weight around or doing anything illegal or unethical. I'm talking about being someone who understands how the world works and makes it work for him. Nobody's sucker. A guy who knows his way around.

So when I walk past a mirror and look at my reflection, I do not see the eyes of a killer. I know there is nothing murderous there, in the mirror. It's just me, Joe. That's what I see.

But if I stop for a while and look deeper, what then? What trace is there of all that time I spent being a wiseguy? Who is staring back at me as I stand there? Whose eyes are those, exactly?

Maybe I ask myself, is there something different about this guy in the mirror?

Maybe the answer is, yeah, a little different.

APPENDIX

TRANSCRIPTS FROM UNDERCOVER SURVEILLANCE AUDIO

The audio CD enclosed in this book includes conversations between FBI Special Agent Joseph Pistone and Mafia made man Lefty "Two Guns" Ruggiero. Agent Pistone secretly recorded these conversations during a particularly tense period of his 6-year undercover operation infiltrating the Bonnano crime family in New York City, in which he was known to the Mafia as jewel thief Donnie Brasco.

These conversations all pertain to the same thing: "sit-downs" (meetings) between Lefty Ruggiero and Mafia leaders to discuss whether or not to whack Donnie Brasco for alleged indiscretions against the Mafia. The sit-downs eventually led to a meeting in which Donnie was sent for and then grilled for several hours regarding his legitimacy. He could have easily been killed at that meeting. But he survived, and ultimately sent more than one hundred wiseguys to jail.

TRACK ONE
Introduction by FBI Special Agent Joseph Pistone

TRACK TWO

Louise: Hello?

Donnie Brasco: Louise?

Louise: Donnie?

Donnie Brasco: Yeah.

Louise: Listen, he's not here now but he said that, uh, he was just at some kind of a meeting.

Donnie Brasco: Okay.

Louise: And, a very important meeting and he wants you to call him every hour until you get him.

Donnie Brasco: Okay.

Louise: Because it's important.

Donnie Brasco: All right.

Louise: All right?

Donnie Brasco: Okay.

Louise: Okay. Thanks. Bye.

Donnie Brasco: Bye-bye. [Hangs up.]

Donnie Brasco: This call was made on March 26th, 1981. Call was made to the resident Bennie Ruggiero at the telephone number 212-962 [audio off then on]. Female speaking identified as Louise Ruggiero, wife of Bennie Ruggiero.

TRACK THREE

Lefty Ruggiero: Yeah, yeah. You know, let me tell you somethin'.

Donnie Brasco: What?

Lefty Ruggiero: This whole fuckin' conversation . . . the last fifteen, forty-five minutes is all based on you.

Donnie Brasco: What's the matter now?

Lefty Ruggiero: Hey, Donnie, Donnie, come off your fuckin' high horses. Let me tell you somethin'. Now listen to me carefully.

Donnie Brasco: I'm listenin'.

Lefty Ruggiero: You're gonna listen. I had a four-and-a-half-hour meeting about you again, again today.

Donnie Brasco: For what?

Lefty Ruggiero: Donnie, don't say for what.

Donnie Brasco: Well, Left, you know, you, you say don't say for what. How do I know—I don't even know what you're talkin' about.

Lefty Ruggiero: Oh, oh. Who else is involved but Mirra?

Donnie Brasco: Well, what's this guy want? What, you know.

Lefty Ruggiero: He don't want nothin'. What'd I tell you, you son of a bitch, that you got me aggravated, about this Rocky?

Donnie Brasco: What about him?

Lefty Ruggiero: All right? Rocky admitted that you made $250,000 in excess amount of money and . . . I'm not gonna bring it on my phone, I'm not burnin' my phone up and you know what I'm talkin' about, that you took $125,000 off him. I could. . . .

Donnie Brasco: From where?

Lefty Ruggiero: From—you say from where? Donnie, Donnie, Rocky—I went at Mirra to that . . . trouble. It's another big sit down . . .

Donnie Brasco: Now, you, who do you believe? You believe him or you believe me?

Lefty Ruggiero: Let me tell you somethin'. How many times that you was in the, in the, in the, in the Cecil's?

Donnie Brasco: How many times I been at Cecil's?

Lefty Ruggiero: Yeah.

Donnie Brasco: I was there, like, two, two, three times.

Lefty Ruggiero: You said it though, you told me once you was there.

Donnie Brasco: No, no. I told you the once I worked there. I said—I told you I was. . . .

Lefty Ruggiero: I asked you a question the first time. You said at the door once but you were there two, three times.

Donnie Brasco: Yeah.

Lefty Ruggiero: Okay. All right, then. Now, you—Rocky admitted, admitted that the bosses, yeah. I won that decision because the guy had no right to go at him, Mirra. He's on the payroll there. You know, let me tell you something, uh, my friend, let me tell you something, I had a big fight with Sonny over you today, uh, about a half hour ago, an hour ago.

Donnie Brasco: About what?

Lefty Ruggiero: Why? Because they went there, I told you to go to Rocky, you says no.

Donnie Brasco: I didn't say no.

Lefty Ruggiero: No. You did—I told you to tell him to get away from, get away from that son of a bitch. Did you—did you bring him in town?

Donnie Brasco: Who?

Lefty Ruggiero: You.

Donnie Brasco: What do you mean, did I bring him in town?

Lefty Ruggiero: Did you bring Rocky in town?

Donnie Brasco: Yeah, he come up there. Why?

Lefty Ruggiero: You, you, you, he, he come up there. Why?

Donnie Brasco: You know, you, you're talkin' in circles. I don't know what. . . . First, tell me what the argument was over.

Lefty Ruggiero: Forget about argu. . . . You're gonna be sent for—you're gonna be sent for. And I promise you one thing. Nothin's gonna happen to you 'cause I stuck up for you all the way. Let me tell you another thing. . . .

Donnie Brasco: Who did Rocky—who did Rocky tell that I made $125. . . .

Lefty Ruggiero: Anthony Mirra, that you shook him down, you made it in fuckin' junk money. Hey, look, hey, look, I'm fed up with this bullshit already!

Donnie Brasco: What, what, I didn't hear you. What?

Lefty Ruggiero: On junk money.

Donnie Brasco: Junk money?

Lefty Ruggiero: Yeah. That's right. Rocky admitted this. Could you prove different?

Donnie Brasco: Left, anything I ever did, you know about. What are you talking about, junk money?

Lefty Ruggiero: What are we gonna do about Rocky? Well, what, what, what are we gonna do with Rocky? Where did I ever see Rocky outside of Miami Beach that you cut up any money, where have I cut any money with you in Miami Beach?

Donnie Brasco: Never.

Lefty Ruggiero: Thank you. But you admit all this.

Donnie Brasco: I admit what?

Lefty Ruggiero: Okay. You admit all this?

Donnie Brasco: What? I never cut any junk money with him.

Lefty Ruggiero: All right, forget it. Any money with Rocky, you cut any money?

Donnie Brasco: No.

Lefty Ruggiero: No? You, you're sure about this?

Donnie Brasco: Left.

Lefty Ruggiero: Alright, let me tell you something. Sonny's fed up. I'll tell ya. He's fed up. He believes that I'm hiding from him. I . . .

Donnie Brasco: What, he thought the money?

Lefty Ruggiero: Forget about that. Uh. Anthony Mirra's men. I have—Let me tell ya. I, I just got . . . I just got off the table, you have no . . .

Donnie Brasco: Well, who did Rocky, who did Rocky tell that I cut $125,000?

Lefty Ruggiero: Anthony Mirra, and he went back to his people and he brought the people back and he admitted to them.

Donnie Brasco: Who did? Rocky?

Lefty Ruggiero: Right.

Donnie Brasco: To who?

Lefty Ruggiero: Anthony Mirra and his men. Don't you understand English?

Donnie Brasco: He's a lyin' son of a . . .

Lefty Ruggiero: You fuckin' jerk off!

Donnie Brasco: He's a lyin' son of. . . . He's lyin', Left.

Lefty Ruggiero: I don't give a fuck. He's, I know he's lyin'.

Donnie Brasco: So what are you hollering at me for?

Lefty Ruggiero: What am I hollering at you for?

Donnie Brasco: Yeah.

Lefty Ruggiero: Because I told you to do this a long time ago, and you didn't do it. You're fuckin' lacksed. Now, forget about you and Rocky. I went at the fuckin' captains. I'm in trouble today. Now we're goin' right to the top. This is what the fuck.

Donnie Brasco: Well, he's a liar. I never cut any junk money up with him.

Lefty Ruggiero: Yeah, but your word don't fuckin' count.

Donnie Brasco: Huh?

Lefty Ruggiero: Mirra's word counts.

Donnie Brasco: Why does his word count?

Lefty Ruggiero: Why? Because he put words in the guy's fuckin' mouth that his captain said it was, you was there, he seen you three, four times at the door.

Donnie Brasco: Who?

Lefty Ruggiero: You know you're a son of a bitch.

Donnie Brasco: No, I'm saying, you mean. . . .

Lefty Ruggiero: Leave it alone. We're handling it. We're going right to the top.

Donnie Brasco: Lefty, I was at that door, I was at that door once.

Lefty Ruggiero: All right. That's all. And you never got a dime for it?

Donnie Brasco: Never got a dime. I told you. What, am I gonna lie to you?

Lefty Ruggiero: Sonny took my fuckin' word for it.

Donnie Brasco: Huh?

Lefty Ruggiero: Sonny took my word.

Donnie Brasco: What am I, gonna lie? You want me to call Sonny and tell him?

Lefty Ruggiero: No, you're not supposed to lie. You never lied. I believe in you. And I turned around and says one thing. I had a big fight with Sonny after the whole conversation.

Donnie Brasco: What, Sonny don't believe it?

Lefty Ruggiero: Yes, he. Why don't you fucking—you're, you're, Donnie, you gonna keep your fuckin' mouth shut?

Donnie Brasco: All right. Go ahead.

Lefty Ruggiero: All right. Just calm down and keep your fuckin' mouth shut 'cause I'm going through this here. I went at them. I got off the table from—you know, they had people from Canada down to represent this mother's debt over you. When I blew my fuckin' top and got off the table, when I went at Mirra at the end of the bar, we're off the table, they come off the table—his captain that put his hand on me and said 'Lefty.' 'Get your hand off me!' I says. He says, 'You know what you're talking about?' ' Get your fuckin' hand off me!' The whole joint heard it. You understand?

Donnie Brasco: Oh yeah.

Lefty Ruggiero: Get your fuc—I'm no fuckin' mutt. He's a mother-fucking liar!

Donnie Brasco: He is.

Lefty Ruggiero: But, Donnie, you got nothin' to say about it.

Donnie Brasco: Oh, I could . . .

Lefty Ruggiero: I'll take it now.

Donnie Brasco: I could tell, tell you he's a liar.

Lefty Ruggiero: Ain't the question. You ain't gonna tell me nothin'. You ain't tellin' me nothin'. I won you and I'm gonna keep you.

Donnie Brasco: Well, that's right.

Lefty Ruggiero: Right. I'm not givin' you up and so is Sonny. Goin' all the way. I didn't like the last remark, that Sonny says, well, we, we own Donnie and we givin' up Rocky. 'No, you give up my prick!' I says. Now, I gotta be down there quarter to twelve tomorrow.

Donnie Brasco: Good.

Lefty Ruggiero: They won't be there tomorrow. I went at Anthony Mirra tonight.

Donnie Brasco: What's with, you know, what's with this guy?

Lefty Ruggiero: Look, Donnie, Donnie, you, you don't understand the ins and outs of anything. It's goin' to the top—let me tell you somethin'. If you can afford to go through—that we tying people up. I mean, I got sent for today. I got sent for. I got back by seven o'clock, for this fuckin' meeting. I got my wife up . . . in case you call, call, keep on calling.

Donnie Brasco: I did. I called you every hour, did she tell ya?

Lefty Ruggiero: All right. Well, let me tell you somethin'. Donnie, Rocky, the statement I made and I'll tell you one fuckin' thing.

Donnie Brasco: Was he there?

Lefty Ruggiero: I gonna give up my wife, I'm gonna give up my wife and give up my children and everything. I turned around and told Mirra, in front of witnesses, here's motherfuckin' Rocky, I win this decision. . . . Oh, he's on the payroll out there, you know. That's why Sonny don't want a fuckin' part of you any more.

Donnie Brasco: Why?

Lefty Ruggiero: Why? He's on the payroll out there.

Donnie Brasco: Who is?

Lefty Ruggiero: I told you. Anthony. He's out there every day. I told you which— See? This is what was bothering Sonny. Lefty, did you say 'I'm gonna lie to my man. Now, why did he pick it up? What is he afraid of? What's in the back of his head?' You see, you're givin' people fuckin' doubts. Now, Anthony Mirra's on the fuckin' payroll of the whole fuckin' organization. He's runnin' the joint. He's out there from 8 to 3 in the afternoon. He's got Joe, Joe, uh. . . . He's got every wiseguy out there. Right? Now, they put words in the guy's mouth. The guy is scared. [inaudible] You didn't call him. So there's your answer. Now, you were gonna put me in fuckin' trouble because I told you to do something— Remember I told you last night, what'd I tell you this morning? Forget about last night. Donnie, what the fuck am I comin' to Miami for? What am I, an impressionist? I finished Jerry . . . out there. He's got 50 things goin' while he's over there in Vegas now. He gets $5,000 a day. . . . What have I got with you, Donnie? I got nothin' but aggravation. You're tryin'. You're tryin' what? The guy admits, and there's two men there. They got the guy but they can't get the satisfaction from Rocky. They can't get the satisfaction. I have to get it.

Donnie Brasco: Well, he's a liar and Mirra's a liar.

Lefty Ruggiero: No, you, no, you can't—your word don't count? Because I'll tell you why.

Donnie Brasco: Why?

Lefty Ruggiero: Rocky already said it.

Donnie Brasco: What, well, he's, cause, just 'cause he said it first?

Lefty Ruggiero: No, well, he said it first. Your word don't count, my man.

Donnie Brasco: Why?

Lefty Ruggiero: Why? I told you. You see? I need a backup man. Now it's beyond Sonny. It's out of Sonny's hands now, your case. I warned you, I'm not givin' you up. I die with you.

Donnie Brasco: So what do we do now?

Lefty Ruggiero: What do ya do?

Donnie Brasco: We just let this guy bullshit and lie all, to everybody?

Lefty Ruggiero: You didn't hear the question. You still fuckin' don't understand. In other words, I wanted you to come in but I didn't want to scare you from comin' in.

Donnie Brasco: Hey, Left, I ain't afraid of anybody.

Lefty Ruggiero: I don't give a fuck but you can't help me out.

Donnie Brasco: I ain't afraid of anybody.

Lefty Ruggiero: You can't help me out. I have to handle it. Without you.

Donnie Brasco: And I ain't afraid of Mirra, either.

Lefty Ruggiero: Ah, look, let me tell you somethin'.

Donnie Brasco: What?

Lefty Ruggiero: Get off your fuckin' high horses and call me back later.

Donnie Brasco: No, no, I want. . . .

Lefty Ruggiero: You're fuckin' aggravating me.

Donnie Brasco: No, no, I wanna talk to you now.

Lefty Ruggiero: No.

Donnie Brasco: All right. I'll listen to you. Go ahead. I'll listen.

Lefty Ruggiero: You wanna listen to me?

Donnie Brasco: Yeah, I'll listen to you. Go ahead.

Lefty Ruggiero: When I got sent for today, Sonny didn't tell me what he wanted to talk about. He said 'I want you to stay here.' I said, 'Why?' He said 'Sally is coming down.'

Donnie Brasco: Uh huh.

Lefty Ruggiero: Well, forget about names.

Donnie Brasco: Yeah, all right. I know what you're talkin' about.

Lefty Ruggiero: He's comin' down.

Donnie Brasco: I know what you're talkin' about.

Lefty Ruggiero: And so, so what, well, it's . . . birthday. You got to be kidding, I got three dollars in my pocket. What the fuck I gotta be over there? I'll wish him luck when I see him.

Donnie Brasco: Yeah.

Lefty Ruggiero: I'll have a drink with him Saturday.

Donnie Brasco: Yeah.

Lefty Ruggiero: All of a sudden, Mirra walked in, two guys, and they all case [inaudible] he don't warn me. What's goin' on? Then when I blew my fuckin' top, he says, 'You know, you're supposed to listen.' 'I listen to my prick,' I says. I don't listen to nobody. And then I went through the whole spiel. And I stuck to my guns. Now, he says, 'What are you gonna do?' No, this is principle's sake. Another main guy, like Sonny, said, 'Lefty, stick to your guns, I'll go back and tell my guy in the can.'

Donnie Brasco: Yeah.

Lefty Ruggiero: I said, I'm goin' right to the top with it, ain't the idea. Here is the gimmick with you. You're ready to fuckin' Miami. Yes, I proud, I bragged about it. But he's ready to barter. You can put us there. Forget about what you did or what you didn't do. The gimmick is this. You're . . . he thinks you made it . . . then when Rocky, they got Rocky down with three witnesses, heavyweights, they scared him. You know? You put a poor gun to a guy's head. . . .

Donnie Brasco: I know what you're . . . . Right. Okay. Yeah.

Lefty Ruggiero: Okay. But here's the gimmick with Sonny. I warned you three months ago, five months ago, I admitted about the $1,000 that I borrowed from but.

Donnie Brasco: Yeah.

Lefty Ruggiero: I had to admit that and lower my standards.

Donnie Brasco: Yeah.

Lefty Ruggiero: Okay. I told you to call the guy up. You says fuck 'em. So between you and him, there's somethin' wrong. I can't figure. I'll tell you one thing, I didn't drink. I drank a few drinks but I don't want any part of it. Between you givin' that up and me tellin' you.

Donnie Brasco: But what, what's. . . .

Lefty Ruggiero: Just a minute.

Donnie Brasco: All right. Go ahead.

Lefty Ruggiero: Just—no, you ain't gonna go on.

Donnie Brasco: No, I said go ahead.

Lefty Ruggiero: It's got the, it's got to be—everything's gonna boil up to a head. Donnie, from you puttin' 'em there, remember what you're sayin' now. I never brought that out. You come in with him, you gave him the job. Somebody put him there. The guy that put him there was on the boat. The guy is a federal stool pigeon. Let's put that that way. They don't know that there yet. They don't know that there yet. They don't know that there. As long as you don't say anything. Let's cut to a head, because, for . . . my friend, I might go to jail for the rest of my life. Now. Rocky come in through you. Now, when the meeting comes up again, how I know Rocky is through you.

Donnie Brasco: That's right. And I met him down there.

Lefty Ruggiero: You met him down there. How did you meet him?

Donnie Brasco: I met him at the bar.

Lefty Ruggiero: Right.

Donnie Brasco: I told you that.

Lefty Ruggiero: All right. The guy belong to you?

Donnie Brasco: Left, you know. . . .

Lefty Ruggiero: I asked a question, Donnie. Look, let me tell you something, I'm gonna go through this thing. Don't think this meeting is tomorrow, next week. In other words, I have to fly down if he wants me to. I don't like Sonny's words or what he did.

Donnie Brasco: Yeah.

Lefty Ruggiero: In other words, he wants to give up Rocky for you. No, I won't do that. Let's find out the fuckin' truth of what's goin' on 'cause I'm in the fuckin' middle. Not Mirra. Mirra's a motherfuckin' swindling bastard.

Donnie Brasco: That's right. He is.

Lefty Ruggiero: Well, that's beside the point. But I'm, I'm caught in the middle. Listen. I'm askin you a question. You met him down where? Donnie, let's go back to the beginning, Donnie.

Donnie Brasco: Left, I told. . . .

Lefty Ruggiero: Donnie, I told ya, I put up my life for you.

Donnie Brasco: I met him in, in Lauderdale at, at the bar down there. I told you that. At Pier 66.

Lefty Ruggiero: Donnie, Donnie, Donnie, we ain't saying different. Why would the man—you know, you got a problem because you're not gonna be there. You ain't got no problem. The man admitted you made $250,000.

Donnie Brasco: Because, like you said, Mirra put the words in his mouth.

Lefty Ruggiero: Mirra put it in?

Donnie Brasco: That's why.

Lefty Ruggiero: Could you prove it?

Donnie Brasco: How am I gonna prove it?

Lefty Ruggiero: Let me tell you somethin'. I can prove it.

Donnie Brasco: It's my word against his.

Lefty Ruggiero: No, no. Can I tell you somethin'?

Donnie Brasco: How?

Lefty Ruggiero: I could prove it.

Donnie Brasco: How?

Lefty Ruggiero: How? Donnie, Donnie, listen to me, he, he told his people that he, he just made $125,000. Donnie, you gotta remember one thing, do you trust me?

Donnie Brasco: Of course I do.

Lefty Ruggiero: Okay. Good enough. All right. I'll take it from there. If—I'm gonna make Sonny . . . a lot of money. I'll handle it.

Donnie Brasco: Of course I trust you. What do you, you know?

Lefty Ruggiero: Okay. Well, you're not gonna be in the picture.

We're gonna be in the picture.

Donnie Brasco: Well, let me ask you this question now. . . .

Lefty Ruggiero: I asked you one question. . . .

Donnie Brasco: Well, let me ask you the question. Do you think I made that kind of money with him?

Lefty Ruggiero: No.

Donnie Brasco: And not, and not give. . . .

Lefty Ruggiero: I said no, and Sonny said the same thing. But let me ask you a question.

Donnie Brasco: What?

Lefty Ruggiero: I'm gonna tell you, I, I'm gonna go all the way . . . but I have to go my own route. You sure this guy—forget about it, let me. . . .

Donnie Brasco: I'm sure he's okay, is that what you're talkin' about?

Lefty Ruggiero: No, I, no. No. He can't be okay. He's a, he's a fuckin' stool pigeon bastard. I'll tell you why. Why would he rat you out?

Donnie Brasco: Hey, I, because, probably he's scared of Mirra.

Lefty Ruggiero: Scared of Mirra?

Donnie Brasco: Like you said.

Lefty Ruggiero: Don't call Sonny up.

Donnie Brasco: Huh?

Lefty Ruggiero: Don't, don't call Sonny up.

Donnie Brasco: All right. I won't.

Lefty Ruggiero: I'm gonna ask for permission. I don't, I, uh. . . .

Donnie Brasco: That's the only reason. I, I'm sure the guy's okay.

Lefty Ruggiero: Hold on for a minute.

Donnie Brasco: 'Cause I know the guy did stuff, you know, but I don't know why he would say, unless Mirra made him say it, that we cut up uh $250,000 in junk money.

Lefty Ruggiero: I'm talkin' to my wife because, I can't get no fuckin' satisfaction in Brooklyn. I can't. You understand? I can't get no satisfaction in Brooklyn. The only satisfaction I got, I gave up everybody I don't give a fuck for nobody.

Donnie Brasco: Well, Sonny believes us so, I mean, that's, you know.

Lefty Ruggiero: Sonny wanted to make a compromise, but then he says, when I blew my fuckin' top, now hold off, he wanted to give up Rocky for you. Now, I, you know, I'd go all the way and die with the kid and that's it. The guy held up. Well, again I'll try to mention it. Go all the way, Lefty, 'cause I'll, I'll make a trip.

Donnie Brasco: All right. I know what you're talkin' about. I know what you're talkin' about.

Lefty Ruggiero: Ain't nobody havin' you. That ain't the question.

Donnie Brasco: Hey, I don't want no part of Mirra.

Lefty Ruggiero: Ain't the question.

Donnie Brasco: What am I gonna do with him?

Lefty Ruggiero: This fucker . . . $250,000. And he injected the word. In other words, I want this guy's head. I got to have his head 'cause he's lookin' for mine.

Donnie Brasco: I know.

Lefty Ruggiero: The only thing . . . he tells his people. He says, 'You know, I live in Lefty's building, I live on the sixth floor, Lefty lives on the eighth.' He says, 'When I got no coffee, stuff like that. . . .'

Donnie Brasco: He said what?

Lefty Ruggiero: Coffee and stuff like that.

Donnie Brasco: Oh, yeah, yeah, yeah.

Lefty Ruggiero: Butter. So, in front of his men, he says, 'Well, some mornings I'll stop and knock on Lefty's door.' I says, 'I'll tell you what, Anthony Mirra, you stop at my door I'll shoot you right in the head 'cause you're not my friend.' Youse all understand that there? In other words, if I catch . . . now, I injected that.

Donnie Brasco: Yeah.

Lefty Ruggiero: Then when I catch you by my door I'll kill ya. You have no right to be at my door. He . . . you put me on a cross, you can definitely. . . .

Donnie Brasco: And then he wants a, yeah.

Lefty Ruggiero: So let me—Sonny Black collected that remark.

Donnie Brasco: Yeah.

Lefty Ruggiero: In other words, you come near me then you're my, you're my enemy. You can't do that. That's what you're good for, boxing people in. You can't box me in. I injected that in front of everybody. Now, in case I catch him in my hallway, I'll drag him over to my door and that's it. But the question is this, my man. I want Rocky. I want Rocky bad. No question about it. I told you. That day I got up bad, had a hangover and I was on, on this couch all night. Louise was . . . . Got up this morning, I says, son of a, laying out the window, quarter after nine, I says, man, I says, this is gonna be a bad day.

Donnie Brasco: You knew, huh?

Lefty Ruggiero: I knew it. I didn't know what it was about.

Donnie Brasco: Yeah.

Lefty Ruggiero: I had about six dollars in my pocket or sixteen dollars, whatever.

Donnie Brasco: What, all this happened today?

Lefty Ruggiero: All day. No, I went to Brooklyn. So Sonny, I, I left there at a quarter to one. Sonny says, 'Uh, come back,' he says, 'It's Booby's birthday.' Ah, come on, Sonny, I says, I, I can't even buy a drink. Come back, come back, come back. He don't answer me, right?

Donnie Brasco: Yeah.

Lefty Ruggiero: He knows he's got an appointment. By hook or crook, I wound up back in Brooklyn. There was a meeting. And that was it.

Donnie Brasco: Well, how does Sonny stand tonight, with us?

Lefty Ruggiero: Where does he stand? He's not giving you up. Not giving you up. But he's not on your side.

Donnie Brasco: Huh?

Lefty Ruggiero: He's not on your side. He's not on your side, I'll tell you that much. No, he's not on your side. In other words, anything happens, I take the weight. He's goin' for me but he's not on your side. I'm telling you that right now. He's not even on my side because everybody heard, give up one, you don't want him, you don't want Rocky, no, I don't want Rocky. But he can't have him. But I said what I had to say. The joint is bugged. I go, I put two bullets in his eyes and I specify what kind of a caliber it's gonna be. See, I don't care. Let me tell you somethin'. They walk the streets with a, can I tell you, I'm proud. My family will be proud. But this is ridiculous. That's what I meant.

Donnie Brasco: Now, why does this, why does this guy wanna, you know, start. . . .

Lefty Ruggiero: He wants you bad.

Donnie Brasco: Well, what's he think?

Lefty Ruggiero: Because Rocky says you got Miami knocked up. So when I went at him, I said, 'Well, I, I, I, I took down part of that money?' 'No, I didn't say that there.' Well, I'll tell you what. . . .

Donnie Brasco: That's what would be implicated, right? Because if I'm with you, you're gonna get some of it, right?

Lefty Ruggiero: Right. But I don't know anything about it.

Donnie Brasco: Now, do you think that, that if I. . . .

Lefty Ruggiero: Well, Rocky, three years ago, I never met Rocky three years ago.

Donnie Brasco: That's right. I didn't even know him three years ago.

Lefty Ruggiero: Well, this is what we're gonna bring out. This is . . . you got to come in to see Sonny. I don't want you to come in. I don't want you unless I give you, believe me, bottom line, that you comin' in for me. Nobody else. And I'll tell you another thing, though. Sonny could have a, a, this I accept, Sonny can call you on the side 'cause he maybe figures I put words in your mouth but I'm no Anthony Mirra. I injected that. Remember that there.

Donnie Brasco: Yeah.

Lefty Ruggiero: Well, this is all it's about. But I can't believe what this man is doin'. I can't. I really don't. Well, I blame one thing. Sonny wants no problems.

Donnie Brasco: Yeah, well, you know.

Lefty Ruggiero: No, no, let me tell you somethin'. I kept my own weight, my man. That's it, pal. I got a lotta strength when I want to use it and I used it today 'cause he didn't believe what I did and that ain't gonna happen to me. Nothing's gonna happen to me 'cause I got balls enough to know what I'm doin'. 'Cause when I inject, I didn't inject in front of them. They heard the conversation. When they come over, I said, we're discussing something. I didn't say I'm arguing. But they heard the argument. I called them over there, but now, he had it all wrong because, it's all friends of ours there.

Donnie Brasco: Yeah.

Lefty Ruggiero: Well we debate.

Donnie Brasco: You got another one, another meeting tomorrow?

Lefty Ruggiero: No, I got no meetings tomorrow. I got, I'm busy all day tomorrow. With no money, nothing.

Donnie Brasco: I mean, was it settled or wasn't settled or. . . .

Lefty Ruggiero: It was settled. I'm going to the top with you. Forget about it. Going right to the top, my man. No, you're not settled. Lotta trouble. See, you're [inaudible], you'll be [inaudible], I'll win the situation. But the trouble you havin' amongst ourselves.

Donnie Brasco: Yeah, I know what you're talkin' about.

Lefty Ruggiero: No, you don't know. Cause let me tell you why. One guy's gonna turn around, Donnie, that's why I say this here, to you. One guy's gonna check both of yous out.

Donnie Brasco: Hey, Left, you know they got no problem checkin' me out.

Lefty Ruggiero: I ain't—could I tell you somethin'? I'm just—I don't give a fuck. If you did somethin' wrong in life, it's for me to handle. And Rocky, for me to handle. But Mirra cannot handle it. Sonny knows what he's doin'. He knows what he's doin'. I'm only sayin' one thing. That, get off your fuckin' ass and I'll tell ya. You see, Donnie, I'm gonna say it once more and I ain't gonna say it no more. You, you come at me a couple of times, see, Booby made three strikes with me. See how much I love Booby? I know Booby a lot more than I know you, right?

Donnie Brasco: Of course.

Lefty Ruggiero: Booby can't come at me no more. You come at me twice. You don't even realize when you come at me.

Donnie Brasco: I don't, I don't, I don't mean to come at ya but, you know. . . .

Lefty Ruggiero: I asked a question. You don't even know it, do you?

Donnie Brasco: No, I don't.

Lefty Ruggiero: Okay. Well, I do. You got one more strike with ya. Not that I'm gonna hurt you or, or hurt Booby, but you can never come at me again after the third time. That's the type I am. I hold everything against. I—forget about, uh, the two strikes you got, I got against you. Like, uh, 'Get your own bag' or somethin' like that. No. I never did it. When I'm with a man, I jump for him. I think before he thinks. And that's why I become successful. You know, not with no money. Manhood, respect from the family, respect from my friends, respect from my children, respect from my wife when she walks the streets, yes, I see—even the niggers respect my wife when she walks. Pretty woman. I know that there. You did it twice. See, Booby may . . . Sonny knows. I, I put it on record with Sonny about Booby. Now, he must a grabbed him. But as far as you. You're my man. I allow. You can. You can. When your man is there, I come first because see what I'm doin' now? You don't know when I'm going through, right? See, like you say, you was just about to say somethin' to me. You jumped the gun.

Donnie Brasco: When?

Lefty Ruggiero: Well, all, you know, you come at me. You know what's goin' on today?

Donnie Brasco: What?

Lefty Ruggiero: What took place today. . .?

Donnie Brasco: What?

Lefty Ruggiero: About you? I mean, you don't—I, I was tryin' to puts words in your mouth. Do you know what through today? You know what four-and-a-half hours is, sittin' down with politicians. . . .

Donnie Brasco: Oh, I know what, you know.

Lefty Ruggiero: No, you don't know. I, see, the fuckin' trouble with you, you don't know.

Donnie Brasco: Well, you never sit down and explain to me.

Lefty Ruggiero: I can't explain to you.

Donnie Brasco: Well, I know you can't over the phone but.

Lefty Ruggiero: All right. He couldn't. And don't forget, he sat there for three hours, you know.

Donnie Brasco: Who?

Lefty Ruggiero: Sonny. Over you. This is goin' on all day, you know.

Donnie Brasco: Well, what, what do we have to do?

Lefty Ruggiero: Not you—that, that we. You got nothin' to do about it. Now it's outta my hands. I make the decision. He goes to sit down. But it has come back to me and that's it.

Donnie Brasco: Well, when's this thing all gonna end with this guy?

Lefty Ruggiero: It ain't gonna end. It's not—you see, Donnie.

Donnie Brasco: All right. You just gonna keep goin' on.

Lefty Ruggiero: Donnie, my wife is over here, I want to tell you, you gonna play with yourself or somethin' like that. Donnie, you made bad feelings in the sense that, I went at everybody today, I went at everybody. I won half the decision, that I'm a crazy maniac. But the zips, I'm in trouble with them. In other words, I'm down. You're a cop fighter. They put it in your jacket. You understand?

Donnie Brasco: Yeah.

Lefty Ruggiero: Well, this is what the zips said to me today. I defied them. And that's it. I defied them. And for what? My friend, Donnie, and he's tellin' me this, this, and that and what's going on or what ain't going on. You understand what I'm talkin' about?

Donnie Brasco: Yeah, I understand.

Lefty Ruggiero: Well, you, no, you don't. I wish you did. I only wish to God. Let me tell you somethin', my friend. When I walk in that town, when I drop a suitcase, pick it up.

Donnie Brasco: I always do, you know that.

Lefty Ruggiero: Ain't the question. What I'm doin' now, I'm pickin' up my brains now. 'Cause I'm, when I give in to Sonny Black about givin' up one to the other, 'cause I know [inaudible]. See, you're not even—can I ask you a question? You know, I'm repeating myself because uh, I could break this fuckin' . . . I can bang the fuckin' phone and break [inaudible] I don't know what the fuck I'm talkin' about. Can I ask you a question? Why ain't you blowing your fuckin' top about the $250,000 with this? Why ain't you mad at Rocky?

Donnie Brasco: I am.

Lefty Ruggiero: You are?

Donnie Brasco: Well, what'd I just say?

Lefty Ruggiero: You know what I . . . Anthony Mirra today? I gotta bawling out. 'You,' I says, 'I catch you in a fuckin' car with him, I shoot him in the fuckin' head. If you're in the fuckin' way, you die, too.' So [inaudible] you tell that motherfucker, he belongs to me. You don't know, back in Brooklyn [inaudible]. I will refuse. And don't forget. This whole afternoon. You're not allowed to drink in that meeting. Nobody can control me. Now, now I'm blowing my fuckin' top because I can't get, I can't through to you. You're not fuckin', in other words, you didn't turn around and say, 'You.' You know what your fuckin' move was supposed to make? You're supposed to think like me. Know what your fuckin' move is? 'Lefty, I'm comin' in tomorrow.'

Donnie Brasco: Well, you, you. . . .

Lefty Ruggiero: You know what . . . would a been?

Donnie Brasco: You said you didn't want. . . .

Lefty Ruggiero: Just a minute. Let me finish what I'm gonna say. Know what . . . would a been? Okay. You come in to see Sonny, don't come to see me. I wanted you to tell Sonny what, what took place.

TRACK FOUR

Lefty Ruggiero: I met him on a boat. It's a federal boat. I know the boat. I got the pictures. I got pictures that I snapped. I got Chavez as a witness, his sister, uh, his brother-in-law. I got everything. They took pictures of the boat. We all got them. You put them up. I gotta tell the truth. Now, I'm gonna stick up for you all the way. Nothing's gonna happen to you. I promise you that much. [Inaudible] you're victimized. But I cannot send my friend—as much as I hate this motherfucker—I cannot send him down the river. He said at the table today, that Rocky got him out on that job there [Inaudible] more information. Especially when they mention the word junk that involves you. It's about. . . .

Donnie Brasco: They think it's a big score.

Lefty Ruggiero: You know what, I care for you, I'm telling you the truth. I've got to go and see what I gotta do tomorrow. Lay the cards on the table. I'll be . . . I'll be wrong, and I swear that you're innocent.

Donnie Brasco: Well, I am.

Lefty Ruggiero: Well, okay.

Donnie Brasco: You know.

Lefty Ruggiero: And I'll take it from there, pal.

Donnie Brasco: All right.

Lefty Ruggiero: All right.

Donnie Brasco: I'll call you tomorrow.

[hangs up phone]

Donnie Brasco: This recording is the second part of a conversation between S.A. Joseph D. Pistone and Bennie Lefty Ruggiero. The telephone call was made by S. A. Pistone to Bennie Ruggiero at telephone number 212-962 [audio off].

TRACK FIVE

Lefty Ruggiero: What, friend, what happened?

Donnie Brasco: Huh?

Lefty Ruggiero: What happened, my friend?

Donnie Brasco: What? I called, you weren't out there. I talked to Sonny.

Lefty Ruggiero: You talked to Sonny? What about last night?

Donnie Brasco: Last night?

Lefty Ruggiero: Yeah. With the sports? I mean, you know?

Donnie Brasco: I called you this morning.

Lefty Ruggiero: You didn't call me at no. . . .

Donnie Brasco: I know. I missed ya then I called ya at the club.

Lefty Ruggiero: Let me tell ya something. I was at the club at 2:00 this afternoon . . .

Donnie Brasco: What, he didn't tell ya I called you?

Lefty Ruggiero: No, he wasn't there at two o'clock this afternoon.

Donnie Brasco: I called out there at 11, at uh, about quarter after 11. I called the house, nobobdy answered.

Lefty Ruggiero: Let me tell you something, Donnie, the man never told me nothin'. He's playin' games with me. He knows I'm feuding with him, 'cause I don't like what's goin' on.

Donnie Brasco: I called the, I called your house.

Lefty Ruggiero: What, what happened last night, Donnie? I asked you a question.

Donnie Brasco: We got, we got, we got, we got whooped.

Lefty Ruggiero: You got what?

Donnie Brasco: We lost $2,400.

Lefty Ruggiero: You lost $2,400?

Donnie Brasco: Yeah.

Lefty Ruggiero: He knows about it?

Donnie Brasco: Well, I told him, I called out that, that . . . joint. I asked for you and Boots said, uh, you're not there but Sonny's here. So he let me talk to Sonny. So I told him, we lost $2,400. We're in the hole $750.

Lefty Ruggiero: And what'd he say?

Donnie Brasco: He said, well, he said, uh, take it. Take it next week and uh, be careful. I said, that's all?

Lefty Ruggiero: Well, how come he didn't tell me a goddamn thing?

Donnie Brasco: I don't know.

Lefty Ruggiero: Hey, listen. Let me tell you somethin'. You're losing a lot of prestige because I'll tell you why. I've been scheming all day today and it's me to know what I'm scheming about. There's something wrong that you're supposed to call me last night. You know I'm home on Sunday night. You never called about nothin', what we need, what we don't need. You took advantage of the situation.

Donnie Brasco: Well, I called . . . in the morning. I told you what we did.

Lefty Ruggiero: Let me tell you somethin', my friend. I waited till ten minutes to eleven this morning for your phone call.

Donnie Brasco: I just missed you, then, 'cause I. . . .

Lefty Ruggiero: That's not the question, Donnie. Look, I don't particularly care. I'm only hoping you bail it out by next week because we never know over a dime. Because, whatever we owe, next week, everybody's chipping in because this here's a different ball game. I'll send my own men out there.

Donnie Brasco: You're mad at him. Why you get mad at me?

Lefty Ruggiero: I'm mad at you, too, Donnie.

Donnie Brasco: Why do you get mad at me? I figured he, I figured he'd tell you that, that uh.

Lefty Ruggiero: No, he didn't tell me a fuckin' thing, Donnie. He didn't tell me nothin'.

Donnie Brasco: And that I called you, that I'd call you tonight.

Lefty Ruggiero: You just won't call me tonight.

Donnie Brasco: I just woke . . . I'm just sleepy. You just woke me up.

Lefty Ruggiero: That's all bullshit, Donnie.

Donnie Brasco: Why?

Lefty Ruggiero: It is all bullshit. You'll call me tonight. From now on, after the phone call, you don't call nobody from now on. I got, I'm makin' a trip out there and I ain't no bullshit. . . . I'm not feuding with the man. The man knows I'm right.

Donnie Brasco: You just said you was feuding with him, now you say you're not.

Lefty Ruggiero: [Inaudible] I'm feuding because I'm right.

Donnie Brasco: Well, what's goin' on up there?

Lefty Ruggiero: That don't concern you, Donnie. That's the trouble with you, Donnie. You know . . . talkin' about, him and I. You're on . . . arguing with him. At least I give you the satisfaction of me tellin' you I'm arguing with him. He's tryin' to be cute with me. Now he's not comin' out this week with uh, what's his name. When he heard Carmine set it up, he said, 'If you don't go, what am I doing there?' This morning.

Donnie Brasco: Well when's he coming?

Lefty Ruggiero: [Inaudible] out of my business, Donnie! And you don't make no phone calls. It's why I gotta put a stop with you.

Donnie Brasco: What phone calls?

Lefty Ruggiero: In other words, you don't worry about when he's coming or when he ain't comin'. We're gonna argue. We got . . . from now on.

Donnie Brasco: When you. . . .

Lefty Ruggiero: He's treating me like a piece of shit today. Didn't tell me nothing.

Donnie Brasco: Is that my fault?

Lefty Ruggiero: No. You ain't your fault. You were supposed to call me last night, Donnie. Let me tell you somethin', Donnie.

Donnie Brasco: What?

Lefty Ruggiero: Look, let me tell you somethin'. I, I think it's gonna come to a head that, that I think uh, we're gonna, we're . . . break up with him and you all belong to me and my position.

Donnie Brasco: That's all right. I don't care.

Lefty Ruggiero: I'm just telling you. . . .

Donnie Brasco: That's got nothin' to do with me.

Lefty Ruggiero: I'm just telling you now. So just take it easy. You were supposed to call me last night, you never called. It's too hard for you to pick up a phone? I told you one thing. I'm gonna revive what I told you, a, a long time ago.

Donnie Brasco: What?

Lefty Ruggiero: I got to know where I'm at. That's what I'm telling you. As far as I'm concerned you're a hundred percent, a lot of people make a lot of money, aren't there. [Inaudible] you throw a broad at him and he's happy. Now, that's bullshit. You know me, when I go outta town with you.

Donnie Brasco: I know.

Lefty Ruggiero: Oh, you know? That ain't the first time I'm gonna tell ya. I don't follow nobody and I act the part of the man. Don't . . . out at me.

Donnie Brasco: Well, why didn't he tell you I called?

Lefty Ruggiero: He didn't tell me nothin' because he thinks he's King Farouk. Now, your friend's brother, uh, uncle [inaudible].

Donnie Brasco: He ain't my friend.

Lefty Ruggiero: Donnie, you got nothin' to say about this whole situation. I'm just telling you one thing. You tell him you're stuck 750? He tell you go out there next week? That's your business. That's all.

Donnie Brasco: If we get stuck, he gotta come up with the money.

Lefty Ruggiero: He has to come up with it.

Donnie Brasco: I mean, we're, you know, what are we gonna do?

Lefty Ruggiero: He has to come up with it but that ain't the idea. He didn't tell me a goddamn thing. He didn't tell me nothin'.

Donnie Brasco: What time did you get out there?

Lefty Ruggiero: What time I got out there?

Donnie Brasco: Yeah.

Lefty Ruggiero: I was there eleven-thirty.

Donnie Brasco: Well, then you must have just got there. Were you at Bootsie's?

Lefty Ruggiero: Yeah, I was at [inaudible].

Donnie Brasco: You must a just, just walked in after I talked to him.

Lefty Ruggiero: Yeah, but. . . .

Donnie Brasco: And he never said anything to you?

Lefty Ruggiero: [Inaudible] believe me. This man is [inaudible].

Donnie Brasco: Well, what's he, what's he playin' games for?

Lefty Ruggiero: He's playin' games with himself. Everyone's disgusted with him.

Donnie Brasco: I know that. You told me that.

Lefty Ruggiero: The whole world is disgusted with him. What's that got to do with me? I'm not gonna break up Miami. I got, I can get the money. I got access to all kinds of money if I need it for business-wise [inaudible]. I ain't worried about that. But to give it, with this guy, you can't talk to. When [inaudible] Carmine said 'Lefty, what, you're not comin'?'

Donnie Brasco: So Carmine didn't know you weren't comin'.

Lefty Ruggiero: No, I said, 'I'm not going.'

Donnie Brasco: Ah.

Lefty Ruggiero: So he don't wanna go. Carmine.

Donnie Brasco: I don't know what he's doing. He just said to me uh, you know, I told him, I said, tell Lefty I called, you know, and uh, he says, uh, keep in touch. I told him, I said, we got beat . . . the $2,400. I said. . . .

Lefty Ruggiero: Well, that's not what he told me yesterday. He give me an argument yesterday. I don't know what the fuck he put them guys up to.